The Joy of Ministry

The Joy of Ministry

Edited by
JAMES D. JENKINS

ISBN: 0-87148-452-8

CONTENTS

FOREWORD

Ministry . . . exactly what does it mean? There are many definitions of ministry. Much has been said and written about ministry; however, the prodigiousness of it is difficult to capture. We know, without doubt, that ministry involves serving rather than being served. ". . . It is more blessed to give than to receive" (Acts 20:35). To the writers the rewards of ministry far exceed any disadvantage. The blessings of serving (giving of ourselves) are many. Therefore, we have chosen to entitle this book, *The Joy of Ministry.*

The writers of the seven chapters have very capably addressed this subject. Having received the call to the ministry, and through their love for the ministry, dedication, and years of service, they have earned the right to speak of the joy involved in ministry. Each writer has a broad background of ministry and serves in the following areas: Raymond E. Crowley, Assistant General Overseer; Benjamin B. McGlamery, Program Coordinator, Department of General Education; Hoyt E. Stone, Assistant Director, Department of General Education; B. Paul Jones, Pastor Parma Park, Ohio; James A. Cross, Church of God General Advisory Council, Evangelist, Teacher; Harold Stevens, Pastor Lebanon, Ohio; and James D. Jenkins, Director, Department of General Education. Collectively, the writers have more than 225 years in ministry.

The opportunity to serve as editor and to write a chapter in this book has been another joy in my personal ministry. I am grateful to those individuals who have given of themselves to assist me in this project. Special recognition is due Joyce McGlamery, Executive Secretary; Linda Keller, Senior Secretary; and Tammy Hatfield, Secretary—Receptionist.

We are cognizant of the fact that in addressing this subject we have only scratched the surface. I trust this book will stimulate you to discover additional joy in your ministry, for happiness is truly a choice. I pray that your life will radiate the joy of ministry.

Cleveland, Tennessee
October 1985

James. D. Jenkins
Director of General Education

1

THE PULPIT

Raymond Crowley

INTRODUCTION

Much is being written and said today about the hardships and difficulties of ministry. Some ministers are abandoning the call. They are giving up, quitting, or copping out. Others feel put upon, overworked, underpaid, and locked into a burdensome task for which they can find no real answers. So prevalent is this problem that a new term has arisen, one never heard a few years ago, ministerial burnout.

Nevertheless, there seems a need for some words about the positive aspects of ministry, about the joys of ministry. I for one feel the joy of ministry far outweighs the pain. The world yet needs the gospel and those who are called to carry the good news are fortunate men and women in any generation. This is a truth we must never forget.

The joy of ministry may be stated in many ways but, for me at least, there is nothing which places it in perspective better than to consider the eternal nature of the minister's work. I simply could not have made it through life involved solely in secular, materialistic pursuits. I have lived long enough to recognize the disappointment and the fallacy which comes with trust in materialism. I would at this moment be a very unhappy man if I had hope in this life only. The eternity of God and His creation is what makes it all worthwhile. Jesus placed a high premium on the value of one human soul. How can we do any less?

The joyous nature of Kingdom work may be likened somewhat to the sales pyramid schemes of our day, where one becomes involved in the marketing of a product, and then enlists others to do the same, drawing a percentage commission on their labors. As the pyramid grows, it is mindboggling what returns may come to those higher up.

We ministers do not work for financial gain but we are in process of making disciples. We instruct those we win to make other disciples also. This has been going on since Christ first established His church and called and commissioned the twelve. Think what this will mean when the end of the age finally arrives and we stand before the Master. Is it not a joyful thought? Compared to this—the eternal nature of our work—all earthly values waste into ashes. This eternal investment will go on forever.

THE CALL TO MINISTRY

No one can understand the real joy of ministry unless first grasping the significance of what we mean by the specific call of God. Life itself may be viewed as a call, in one sense, because God is Creator and author of life. Every Christian is called to witness, to be salt and light in a world of corruption. But I do not here speak of the call of God in such a general sense: rather, I refer to a specific, individual call for a special task upon this earth. It is in this sense where the joy of ministry has its fountainhead.

The Scriptures remind us that God has always chosen certain people for specific tasks.

God called Abram: "Now the Lord had said unto Abram, Get thee out of thy country, and from thy kindred, and from thy father's house, unto a land that I will show thee: And I will make of thee a great nation, and I will bless thee, and make thy name great; and thou shalt be a blessing: And I will bless them that bless thee, and curse him that curseth thee: and in thee shall all families of the earth be blessed" (Genesis 12:1-3).

Notice some of the things required of Abram in this call. He had to leave his native country, get away from his kindred, forsake his father's house, and go into a strange land. These are not easy requirements by any standard. But look also at the promise. God said He would bless Abram, He would make Abram a blessing to others, He would make Abram's name great, and He would make of Abram a great nation. In fact, God promised that in and through Abram all families of the earth would be blessed.

God's call to Moses was also very specific (Exodus 3). God appeared at a specific time and place, and God manifested Himself in a specific manner, through the burning bush. This was a divine intervention, God moving into the material realm in a tangible, observable fashion. The bush burned but was not consumed. The ground was made holy by the manifest presence of God. Moses was instructed to lead the children of Israel out of Egyptian bondage.

"Who am I, Lord, that I should go unto Pharaoh?" Moses asked (Exodus 3:11).

"Certainly I will be with thee," God replied (Exodus 3:12), going on to add, "Thus shalt thou say unto the children of Israel. I AM hath sent me unto thee. I will be with thy mouth and teach thee what thou shalt say."

Yes, Moses' call was a specific one, for a specific purpose.

Similar incidents are recorded throughout the Old Testament; and, in the New Testament, God called twelve disciples. He chose a variety of individuals—fishermen, a doctor, a tax collector, even one who would in the end betray him. These disciples left their fishnets, their communities, their worldly belongings, everything in order to follow the Master. Such a calling is never easy but, for those who obey, rewards are surely forthcoming.

Georgia Cary, a little lady over in West Virginia, raised three sons who heard the call of God: Lovell Cary has given most of his life to world missions and is presently serving as Assistant Director of the Church of God World Missions Department; Ernest Cary has served as missionary to the Philippines and is now pastoring a Church of God congregation in Ashland, Virginia; And Bob Cary has also served on foreign soil and is now a deputational worker for the World Missions Department. All three of these men will testify of a specific call from God. They have lived out the principles of faithful followers of God and they will tell you that the true rewards and the true joys of ministry are not found in tangible items. They are found in relationship to God and in faithfulness to what He commands.

WHAT MINISTRY REALLY IS

Ministry is a powerful word, a meaningful word, defined as "the act of serving, assisting, or giving aid." Our Lord and His chosen disciples are perfect examples of what it means to minister.

Jesus came into the world to be about His Father's business, to minister to a world in need. At the age of twelve, He went with His parents to Jerusalem. When His parents returned, Jesus tarried behind. They found Him three days later and He said to them, "How is it that ye sought me? Wist ye not that I must be about my Father's business" (Luke 2:49)?

Following His powerful sermon on the mount, during which He had spoken on most every aspect of Christian living and service, Jesus immediately began to minister to those in need. He healed a leper (Matthew 8:2-4). He healed a centurion's servant (Matthew 8:5-13). He healed Peter's mother-in-law of a fever (Matthew 8:14, 15). And He delivered two poor souls possessed with devils (Matthew 8:28-32). Clearly, Jesus saw Himself as more than a teacher. He was a "minister" to human needs.

Matthew's list of our Lord's specific ministries continues in the next chapter. He forgave the sins of one sick of the palsy and healed him (Matthew 9:1-7). He sat at the table with publicans and sinners, silencing the Pharisees who criticized Him with, "they that be whole need not a physician, but they that are sick" (Matthew 9:10-13). He healed a woman who for twelve years had been sick with an issue of blood (Matthew 9:20-22). He raised a girl from the dead (Matthew 9:23-26). And He healed two blind men (Matthew 9:27-30).

What power-packed chapters of ministry!

I fear that in today's world too many preachers have confined ministry to what takes place in the pulpit only. The pulpit is definitely a vital ministry. It is the springboard for ministry. But there is more to ministry than merely delivering a message in a church building where most of the people have been preached to for years. There is a need for ministry and both pastor and laity need to be involved in serving others.

Once again let us look at our Lord's example (Matthew 9:35). Jesus went about all the cities and villages. He was totally and constantly involved in ministry. His ministry was not confined to a pulpit or to one place. He went into all the cities and villages. Everywhere. There is not anything more rewarding than to be involved in ministry. Lasting joy comes when a person can serve the needs of others.

The same verse tells us Jesus extended His ministry wherever He could press open an opportunity to share. We read, "teaching in their synagogues and preaching the gospel of the kingdom." Joy comes when we too utilize every opportunity to teach and to preach the gospel of the Kingdom.

The last statement of this verse tells us our Lord's ministry was filled with miracle after miracle: "healing every sickness and disease among the people." He was touched by those who suffered and He spent much of His time healing them. His was a ministry to human needs.

Jesus was concerned about others. The reason many complain about the burdens of ministry, or about minister's burnout, is that their motives are not right. They are too self-centered and introverted. They live in their own little world, for their own little flock. Jesus said, "The harvest truly is plenteous, but the labourers are few. Pray ye therefore the Lord of the harvest, that he will send forth labourers into his harvest" (Matthew 9:37, 39).

Scriptures confirm that those whom Jesus called were equally involved in ministry: "And when he had called unto him his twelve disciples, he gave them power against unclean spirits, to cast them out, and to heal all manner of sickness and all manner of disease" (Matthew 10:1). Jesus told them, "Heal the sick, cleanse the lepers, raise the dead, cast out devils, freely ye have received, freely give" (Matthew 10:8).

Not only are our Lord's commands relevant for this generation but it is also probably true that there never has been a more opportune time for ministry than this present day. Social commentators, newspapers and magazines, even the daily TV news which comes into our living rooms—all remind us of people who have great needs.

Alcoholism and drug abuse seem to be national diseases, affecting all segments of society. Suicide has become common even among teenagers to such extent that special counseling centers are being established in order to try and stem the tide. Authorities tell us premarital pregnancies are increasing annually and abortions on demand have become a national disgrace, an estimated 1,600,000 unborn babies to be murdered this year alone. The family is under attack on every hand. Divorces are common. All of which should make the full gospel preacher more conscious of ministry opportunity.

Is it not a fact more recognizable than ever that prosperity, abundance of things, what so many refer to as "the good life" will not in and of themselves bring happiness and joy? People need something more real, more enduring, more satisfying. They need the good news of Christ.

What is more rewarding than to see a lost soul repent and come to a knowledge of Christ? What more glorious than to witness one bound by alcoholism set free and delivered through the power of God's Spirit? What joy to snatch a man or woman back from the brink of suicide and to see him or her find meaning and purpose in life through Jesus Christ? To rejoice with the young woman who decides to bring her baby to term and to keep it and raise it in a Christian home? To witness a broken family's restoration to unity and love through the grace of God? Yes, what can be, or could be, more joyful than that? Such is the excitement and the joy of ministry when it confronts the needs of humanity straight forward and without apology.

THE JOY OF DELIVERING THE WORD

The heart of Christian ministry is, and shall ever remain, the Word of God. He who would proclaim the Word must be willing to prepare. There was a time when Bible colleges and seminaries were not so available as they presently are. It has also been true in years past that financing a formal education was more difficult than at present. We have come to a new era for the church. Those who proclaim the gospel, those who minister, must prepare themselves.

This does not mean, necessarily, that every man called to preach will have to be formally trained. It does mean that a higher percentage of those ministers working in the church will need that formal training, just as this is true in every other aspect of life in this late twentieth century. While I readily recognize that God can call any man, from any station of life, to become an anointed preacher of His Word, I also contend that any man truly called of God will do everything within his power to equip himself educationally and intellectually, as well as spiritually, for the task.

Preparation for ministry must center primarily in knowledge of God's Word. "The word of God is quick, and powerful, and sharper than any two-edged sword, piercing even to the dividing asunder of soul and spirit, and of the joints and marrow, and is a discerner of the thoughts and intents of the heart" (Hebrews 4:12). Those who minister must be adept when it comes to understanding, interpreting, proclaiming, and applying the Word. This demands many hours, a continuing regimen of study and personal devotion.

There are no human needs, there are no human problems, to which God's Word does not speak. But there are many needs which cannot be addressed without the Word of God. When everything else fails, turn to the Word and there is the answer.

God's Word has power to erase deep and painful human divisions. I once pastored a church which was almost equally divided. The last pastoral vote was 49 to 51, a percentage which clearly hinted at the division, and the problem was deep-seated and bitter. I tried to mediate differences between the two factions but failed. It looked as if the congregation just could not be brought together again. Then I decided to just preach the Word. Sunday after Sunday the Word of God went forth. I took no sides in the bitter division, just preached God's Word. Grant you, it was slow; but little by little I saw the Word begin to take hold and the lines of division to melt away. The congregation began to blend together more and more. Eventually, harmony was restored through the power of the preached Word.

Preaching the Word will also bring physical and emotional healing. The psalmist prophesied, "He sent his word and healed them" (Psalm 107:20). Jesus enacted this promise when He encountered the faith of the centurion (Matthew 8:8). Men and women today need the strength and the faith which comes from hearing the Word of God. They need healing. They need comfort. They need reassurance which can be found only in the eternal and unchanging Word of the Lord.

Stress, guilt, mental torment, emotional depression—so many things oppress people in our day. But the Scriptures are full of promises which bring peace to the believer. When a called minister prepares and delivers the Word, people have to be helped; and for the minister to witness these miracles of healing and restoration is unspeakable joy. Often these miracles take place right during the sermon itself.

At the Northern Ohio camp meeting, 1985, the night evangelist Raymond Culpepper had to return home for an emergency and I was asked to speak. Sister S. C. Burton had fallen recently, crushing her elbow so severely the doctor had told her she would never be able to use it again in normal fashion. The elbow would be permanently stiff. She would just have to learn to live with it. While the Word was going forth her pastor Robert Bailey looked where she was sitting. She had both arms raised, praising the Lord. God had miraculously healed her.

In Indiana where I was ministering several years ago, something similar happened. One of our ministers, Brother Townsend, had been sent home from the hospital to die. He had resigned his church. The diagnosis, cancer of the prostate, inoperable due to an incurable heart disease. After the Word was preached, I asked Brother Townsend to come forward and the ministers laid hands on him. God instantly healed him. For a time, he reminded me of the man healed at the gate Beautiful in Acts 3, leaping and praising God for joy. Brother Townsend ran around the tabernacle, giving thanks and praise to God.

Several months later I saw Brother Townsend in Chicago. He was pastoring a church, serving as district overseer, and enjoying health and happiness.

During the early sixties, while I was pastoring Canton, Ohio, Sister Crowley became critically ill; and, with the illness, came a deep depression. Her mother Mrs. Grace Milligan came to spend the early weeks of the illness with her. Sister Milligan and I agreed to meet with Frances every morning in the Word and in prayer. Through the assurance of the Word I became more certain of my wife's healing. There were times when I placed the Bible literally upon her body. It was only a matter of days until the illness and depression diminished and soon she was completely healed through the power of God.

The preaching of the Word brings deliverance from sins and burdens. During our pastorate at Canton Sister Crowley started a Sunday school class in a small basement room, with twelve or fourteen people. The class grew, soon had to be moved into the auditorium, and I agreed to teach for Sister Crowley. Her challenge to me was, "If you will teach, then I will visit and bring people to the class."

That class turned out to be one of my greatest lessons on the value of teaching the Word. Many of the people attending the class were troubled people. A large percentage were from broken homes. Some had totally lost their way amid the pressures of city life. Others had financial difficulties.

For one full year I preached/taught from the book of Romans, verse by verse. Each Sunday morning I gave an altar invitation at the end of the teaching session. From one to ten would come forward to seek salvation and help for their troubled lives.

Yes indeed, the Word of God will change lives.

One of the most rewarding incidents to take place during this times was the story of Leonard Morrison. Leonard was a bachelor with no immediate family. Having spent his life as a farm hand, he had no money, no retirement, and was living in the county home. Leonard did have a niece, however, who operated a welfare nursing home, and this niece occasionally brought Leonard to the home for food and change of scenery.

On a bleak, cold, dreary Saturday one of our ministers of visitation, Clara Schrade, stood on the corner of Plain and Spring Streets near that nursing home and felt impressed of the Holy Spirit to go in for a visit. While there she asked, "Would anyone here like to ride our bus to Canton Temple for Sunday school?" Leonard Morrison raised his hand and he came the next Sunday.

After teaching the class I gave the usual invitation and saw this old man make his way slowly down the long aisle to the altar.

"What do you need from the Lord, Sir?" I asked him.

"What you have been talking about."

"Then pray. Ask God to help you."

"I don't know how to pray," Leonard said. "I've never prayed in my life."

I led Leonard Morrison to the Lord that morning and it wasn't long until, with a smile, he said, "It has happened. Just what you were talking about, Preacher. For the first time in my life I am free. Happy."

Several times after that I visited Leonard during illness. He slept in the attic of the welfare "forget-me-not" nursing home—a single bed, a tiny attic room in an old house, cheap khaki shirt and trousers, old brogan shoes. What little spending money Leonard had he received from his niece. His was not what we would think of as much of a life; but, believe you me, what that man found in Jesus Christ remains one of the most rewarding joys of my life.

I look forward to an even more joyous time when I meet Leonard again some day. He will be wearing, not old brogans, but silver slippers. He will be living, not in a county home, but in a mansion. He will be living, not on leftovers, but on heaven's fare, eating from the tree of life. What could be more rewarding? What could bring a man greater joy than such a conversion as that?

THE JOY OF HAVING OBEYED THE CALL

I know a lot of people who are proud to be working for a certain company, a certain firm or business. They will tell you with pride where they are employed, and rightly so. But there is no greater task than that of the God-called minister and we must never cease drawing deep satisfaction from having obeyed God's call.

There are discouraging moments and obstacles, of course, but God never calls a man and then changes His mind. God knows what He is doing. If there is failure, then it is always on the part of man. God never fails.

Some things in my life I have never disliked. First among these is my call to ministry. As far back as I can remember, when I was a little boy, I felt the call of God. After forty-seven years in the ministry—there have been times of discouragement, some dark valleys, some disappointments—but I still do not doubt the call of God. I am answerable to God for that divine call. I owe my all to Him. Whatever I am, or ever will be, I owe to God and to my church; and I find it difficult to describe the deep commitment I feel. Yet I know that herein there is for me a deep sense of joy that stays with me in every moment of my life, something others can't take from me and something life can't deny me. Whatever time I have left on this earth I plan to give it for Christ and His cause. That is happiness and joy which defies words.

Nevertheless, I realize that some good men do grow discouraged. They do turn back and leave the ministry and I often ask myself how and why this can happen. There may be many answers but I am not willing to accept the simplistic idea that they were never really called in the first place. No, the fault is human; and, while I may not have full and perfect explanations as to why this happens, I do have a couple of observations which may be helpful to the readers of this book.

First, some men burn out or fail God from lack of perspective. In other words, they fail to maintain the true, heavenly vision of their calling. When a man's vision narrows until all he sees is his town, his family, his city, his own little world, then carnality is upon him. As carnality grows, so does jealousy and bitterness and disillusionment with what is happening all about. Wrapped up in our own little world we become like people going through a revolving door, round and round, with no progress; and, having thus lost sight of divine purpose, we are easy prey for the enemy of our souls.

When we lift our eyes and take the grand view, when we look on the fields all white unto harvest, when we recognize the greatness of our God and the majesty of what He is doing upon this earth, then comes joy and contentment, a willingness to be patient, and an assurance that God is working in all things both to will and to do of His own good pleasure.

Our product is eternal. Our mission is divine. We must not forget.

I would not make it in the secular world, the world of business, because of a single idea. Where does it all wind up? What is the last chapter? Men amass fortunes and then leave them. We are here today and gone tomorrow. Jesus gave us the true picture: "Lay not up for yourselves treasures upon earth, where moth and rust doth corrupt, and where thieves break through and steal: But lay up for yourselves treasures in heaven, where neither moth nor rust doth corrupt, and where thieves do not break through nor steal" (Matthew 6:19, 20).

In the second place, I'm convinced some men fail because they forget it is the anointing of God which makes the difference. Throughout Scriptures we have many reminders that God anoints certain objects and certain people for His service. God instructed Moses to anoint the altar of sacrifice (Exodus 29:36). The tabernacle was anointed (Exodus 30:26). High priests were anointed (Exodus 29:7). Saul was anointed to be king over Israel and David was subsequently anointed to replace him.

The prophets were anointed. Jesus opened His ministry with these words: "The spirit of the Lord is upon me, because he hath anointed me to preach the gospel to the poor; he hath sent me to heal the broken hearted, to preach deliverance to the captives, and recovering of sight to the blind, to set at liberty them that are bruised" (Luke 4:18).

Throughout the Bible, oil is generally typical of the Holy Spirit, which reminds us of the outpouring of the Spirit on the day of Pentecost, when God anointed His church for its mission on earth. A great harvest of souls was won on the day of Pentecost and, from there, the early Christians went forth with power, witnessing to the resurrected Lord and literally turning the world upside down.

Signs and wonders were wrought by the apostles after this great anointing of Pentecost. They were threatened, beaten, thrown in jail. They had one testimony, "Christ is alive." And they had one answer for those who tried to stop their preaching, "We ought to obey God rather than man" (Acts 5:29).

God still anoints men and women for His work in this day. I have seen singers who were anointed of the Lord. Others, sometimes singing with more harmony, with more talent, even with more professional poise, left a congregation cold and unmoved. Then, that man or woman anointed with the Holy Spirit stood up and things began to happen.

The same is true of preachers. Human words may be beautiful but it takes the power of God's Spirit to penetrate a wicked heart. Human effort may at times move men to human action, or it may, when skillfully applied, move us to emotional tears, but only the divine and miraculous working of God's Spirit will change a life for all eternity.

God's men in the pulpit must never forget that it is the anointing of the Spirit which counts. Before we stand up to preach we must go before God in sincere prayer for His touch. We must receive a message from the throne of God, a message that first burns in our own hearts before it will ever ignite a flame in any hearer. We must be communicators of divine truth, not mere speakers of phrases. It is not really enough just to quote Scriptures. We must make those verses come alive in the arena of life and we must apply them to the hearts and minds of our listeners. Communicators, that is what we are, communicators of truth and of life. To forget this places our work on a carnal level and leaves us powerless to oppose the spiritual powers which presently rule this world.

Yes, Brothers, as so many of us have heard Brother Ray H. Hughes preach and exhort, "The anointing makes the difference." It always will. Remembering this truth, along with keeping the proper perspective or vision, will help us avoid burnout and disillusionment.

CONCLUSION

Ministry in today's world is difficult, no question about that. Burdens are heavy and constant. Stress is ever present. But if you are called, if your motives are right, and if your ambitions are proper, every negative can be dealt with.

There is always a positive way to approach a negative situation and the man of faith must find it. This truth was brought home to me again not long back when I moderated a ministers meeting in the state of Washington. One of the ministers told of a terrible situation at his church. He listed a number of seemingly impossible situations but he then went on to say every problem was an opportunity and he planned by God's help to do something about them. What a positive approach! I have never seen a more vibrant man. He recognized and testified to his divine calling.

The satisfaction, peace, and joy of ministry can last right to the end of a man's life. Unlike other callings, the ministry is something which can go on even after what we normally refer to as retirement. Brother W. R. Marcum pastored the Dane Church in Cleveland, Ohio, for twenty-seven years. He retired from the pastorate at age of 72 and his church was enjoying its greatest growth when he retired. I saw Brother Marcum at the '85 camp meeting in Ohio and he looked as vibrant as ever, still busy as an evangelist.

Health may not permit all to do as Brother Marcum but we can retain the peace and joy of ministry so long as there is breath in our bodies.

Paul H. Walker was one of the great pioneers of the Church of God. From the Dakotas, he was always a strong, rugged individual, preaching right up to the time of his death. Brother Walker's son Don shared with me a few things about his father's last moments. He and Sister Walker were home and he was watching the 6 p.m. news when she noticed something wrong. She called the rescue squad and, when they arrived, there was this conversation:

"I think he's dead," one of the men said.

"He can't be dead," the other responded. "Why, look at him. He still has on his coat and tie. He looks like a general sitting there."

I heard those remarks and remembered the Paul H. Walker I had known for so many years and I thought, "Yes, indeed, a general in the Army of our Lord."

He truly was. And he has now gone on to his reward before the righteous Judge of all the earth.

Investments in materialism, in things of this life, in things earthly—they will fade away. But investment in eternal souls—aw, my Brothers and Sisters, they will not fade. They will pay eternal dividends in New Jerusalem, the city of God.

"Now unto him that is able to keep you from falling, and to present you faultless before the presence of his glory with exceeding joy, to the only wise God our Saviour, be glory and majesty, dominion and power, both now and ever. Amen" (Jude 24, 25).

2

THE PARSONAGE

Benjamin B. McGlamery

INTRODUCTION

It is very presumptuous for anyone to think a minister is a superman, incapable of error. He is a total human being with all the passions and needs common to man. Yet, the minister is a special person, chosen and elected by God for a divine task in this world. Along with this call, Jesus did not promise a path without problems or burdens. The minister realizes this and willingly carries the unique burdens of his church, his family, and his own life.

In carrying out his mission, there are times when the minister experiences worry, frustration, anxiety and feelings of failure, weakness and inadequacy. In addition to these, loneliness and rejection are often with him. Many are the times when the most private feelings cannot be shared with anyone outside his most intimate circle of confidence.

Along with the struggles unique to his labors, the minister learns he has unique strengths from which to draw. Obviously, through prayer and study (the common tools of his trade) he is able to lean heavily on the Lord, finding strength, courage, and insight from the Holy Word. Another great source of strength is friends and colleagues—fellow-ministers who can identify with his trials.

Perhaps the minister's greatest strength, outside the Lord Jesus, comes from his own family. He is strengthened not through words of encouragement alone, but through a close-knit relationship with each family member. In the final analysis, these are the ones who know him best and love him most.

Nolan B. Harmon in his book *Ministerial Ethics and Etiquette* stated that "a minister's relationship to his family is as high and as sacred as that to his church." To this we must agree, adding that it may be even higher for several reasons.

First of all, it is in the home where the minister first learns to serve. According to the Apostle Paul, "If any provide not for his own, and specially for those of his own house, he hath denied the faith, and is worse than an infidel" (1 Timothy 5:8, KJV). Also, in terms of ability, "if a man know not how to rule his own house, how shall he take care of the church of God?" (1 Timothy 3:5, KJV). The minister must accomplish these tasks first, in order to make himself eligible to serve others. His great imperative is to his own family.

It is a sad commentary to hear the lament of any minister who admits, "I saved my church, but I lost my own children." If the minister fails at home, all his successful exploits for the church lose their lustre and significance. While some ministers have failed their families, we know with joy that this is the exception, not the rule. In the parsonage are found first those ideal opportunities and the potential for successful ministry.

The parsonage stands for refuge and contentment. It is the epitome of provision—a provision that is wide in scope. This chapter is an attempt to share a positive word about that provision and to once again emphasize the good fortune of those who are exemplars of grace in the parsonage environment. These words are not offered as the sole authority on the "how to's" of parsonage life. It is an honest portrayal of those aspects of parsonage life which have contributed to the total joy of the writer from both observer and participant viewpoints. Hopefully, total joy in the parsonage can become a reality for you in days ahead.

THE CHALLENGE OF MARRIAGE

The basic prerequisite for joy in the parsonage is that it contain a happily married couple—the minister and his wife. I would be less than honest if I said all ministers' homes are happy homes. If love is in marriage, it is bound to spill over into the church. And if all is well at home, things should go better with the minister and his relationship with his congregation. This is true in any walk of life. If trouble and strife pervade the home atmosphere, these will inevitably spill over into the work area. In regard to the minister, if marriage problems persist, his mind will be encumbered with the troubles at hand and he will not be able to concentrate on the tasks of the ministry. Therefore, for the ministry of any pastor to succeed, the husband/wife relationship must be a proper one.

Of all people the minister should have a loving relationship with his wife. A shaky marriage is the seedbed for the weeds of bitterness and division in the home. The perfect attitude is described by Paul in Ephesians, his exhortation to husbands: "Husbands, love your wives, even as Christ also loved the church, and gave himself for it" (Ephesians 5:25). True love, then, is found in a man who gives himself totally and uncompromisingly to his wife. She in turn is reciprocally submissive to him. Each considers the other's feelings in all areas of life. When agreement cannot be found on certain issues, compromise is a safety valve which will relieve the pressures that occasionally build up.

From the very beginning of the family, God ordained the basic premise of marriage. He said, "Therefore shall a man leave his father and his mother and shall cleave unto his wife: and they shall be one flesh" (Genesis 2:24). This is the cornerstone of marital unity. Whether the family is made up of two or ten members, unity is imperative for the sake of happiness. The prophet Amos asked, "Can two walk together, except they be agreed?" (Amos 3:3). The marriage covenant is no exception. Unity in marriage is the twin of agreement or covenant. Unity is depicted in Scripture as being beautiful and pleasant, like a sweet-smelling fragrance. Not many of us enjoy being around a husband and wife who are constantly fighting and hurling verbal barbs at each other. Neither is it a pleasant sight to see one marriage partner always a passive slave to the wishes and whims of the other. There must be a balanced relationship for any marriage to be happy over the long haul.

The text of the marriage ceremony emphasizes unity as a continuum throughout the lives of the married couple. More is involved, however, than just two people being united together in contract. Many couples are together in the flesh but far apart in the goals of married life. For ideal marriage the real essentials are unity of love and purpose.

In most cases the marriage relationship is not a flawless situation. There are times when problems arise which need quick solutions. The couple which is able to resolve difficulties soon after they appear will continue to have a healthy marriage. Misunderstandings should not be allowed to grow and fester into major obstacles. Out of disagreement must come agreement. As the well-worn cliche advises, "Disagree without becoming disagreeable." "Let not the sun go down upon your wrath" (Ephesians 4:26)—this precept has saved many marriages.

So, we come to the crux of the matter: how can this marital unity be maintained? What are some keys to a successful marriage in the parsonage? There may be complicated situations but the solutions may be surprisingly simple.

A Working Formula

Marriages which work are those in which partners know what makes each other "tick." They have learned how to adjust and to adapt to one another's moods. Most annoying habits and idiosyncrasies are not discovered during courtship. There will always be questions like, "Why does he keep tossing his socks on the floor?" or, "Why does she roll the toothpaste tube in the middle?" or, "Why didn't he tell me that he snores so loudly?" Humorous? Perhaps. But literally marriages have ended in divorce because one marriage partner snored and the other was not able to live with it. However, the man and woman who are bound by love's strong cord will find ways to work through those little annoyances which are common in marriage. Marriage does take work. It must be worked at every day.

Prior to the marriage ceremony couples should come to a mutual understanding, and this must be maintained throughout the marriage. Harmony comes in marriage when partners are willing to be understanding in all things. This is paramount in the life of the minister. The demands of the ministry must be shared and understood. The ministry is not all romance and adventure. There are many unforeseen demands, but these can be worked through by mutual concern for the feelings of each other.

Valuing the Intimate

A time for expressing of feelings for each other is vital to every marriage. Such moments may be referred to as quality time, especially pertinent in the life of minister and wife. Quality time in the ideal sense must be free from distractions.

One minister, griping and complaining about not having enough time with his wife, said, "At times when that phone rings, I'd like to rip it out of the wall."

Perhaps a lot of us are guilty of similar expressions of frustration. There is a better solution. Don't rip the phone out of the wall. Leave it. Just get away to some private place.

Budget time each week to be alone with your wife, a time for sharing what belongs to both of you, intimacy which can brighten up a variety of settings. Some married couples would be surprised at how much joy a meal together can bring to the marriage. Plan a few moments alone, a time for sharing a surprise gift, or for verbally expressing your love and affection. Wives may expect flowers on anniversary day, birthday, and Valentine's Day, but those unexpected gifts of flowers work miracles as well. Short or long trips alone are also excellent times for sharing together. Many subjects can be discussed and problems worked out in the car during travel time. Such time is valuable for sharing hidden thoughts, for determining personal needs, and for exploring unfathomed depths of the personality. It is a time to dream and to make additional plans for the future. For happiness in the parsonage, intimate moments are absolutely essential.

Naturally, this intimacy in marriage includes a healthy sexual relationship, one of those absolute essentials. Sex has been misapplied, distorted, and perverted; and, by some of the misinformed, it has been neglected. There are male and female needs which can be met legitimately only in the marriage bed. To forbid or to ignore these needs is to invite disaster. Due benevolence each to the other is a vital ingredient for a healthy sexual relationship between man and wife.

While some men and women are born to lead celibate lives, most long to share the blissful sexual love of a lifetime marriage partner. The minister is a man with the passions and desires of a normal male. He has needs. And not to be neglected are the needs of the minister's wife. She is the co-worker of the minister, but she is also a female with her own unique set of needs. In one sense she shares her husband with all the church congregation as they admire him and look to him for help. She thus deserves a portion of exclusive response and attention from him. As an equal partner, she deserves time off from her duties as mother and housewife to be alone with her mate. A joyful marriage comes to that couple which considers these needs and takes action to fulfill these needs by the allotment of exclusive quality time. Quality time means privacy, a time when nothing else intrudes.

Another great fallacy in any marriage is for a couple to feel that they can never do anything without the children. This idea has the potential of being very damaging to any marriage. Surely, our children need to feel our love, but this does not preclude the right of spending time away from them. Even in the peaceful confines of the parsonage the pressures of the ministry can impose upon the relationship of the minister and his wife. Happy is that couple which understands the signal indicating the need to "get away from it all" for a while. Jesus, who is our chief example, was Himself a proponent of the retreat.

One ministerial couple experienced a stormy marriage which led to his ineffectiveness as a minister. His exclusive attention to the needs of his church flock so contributed to a strained relationship between him and his wife that his ministry finally terminated at a certain church. This specific case is by no means the exception. When he lost his congregation and almost lost his family too, he took a long hard look at himself. The results of the evaluation were painfully constructive. He realized how much he had failed his wife and family by not giving due benevolence to them. The current situation? Not only has he made a successful comeback in the ministry but his wife says that he is like a new man. No doubt he is a man with a fresh perspective of quality time.

The marriage concept may be made in heaven, but marriages are nurtured and cultivated on earth. They require work and they demand constant attention. When couples—even those in the ministry—fail to take time to work out their unique set of problems, those problems become more pronounced and dissolution of the marriage may be the ultimate result. As we count perfection, perfect marriages may not exist; but mutual goals and purposes for marriage are very real. When these goals and purposes are defined and agreed upon, a couple stands on the threshold of the ideal marriage relationship. Happy is the minister who realizes quality time is necessary for a happy marriage and who is willing to invest as much time as necessary to keep his marriage on track.

Satan would love to destroy the marriages of all ministers. In destroying marriages he cripples good men and he hampers the growth of many churches through all the fallout and negative rhetoric about the minister's problems. Satan is effectively resisted when we cultivate and value our own joyful marriage relationship.

DELIGHTS OF HOME

God meant for the "house" to be a "home" in every good sense of the word. The parsonage is the place where the pastor can find a sure solace after the daily bombardment of church problems and difficulties. In fact, when strength is gained through wonderful home relationships, the problems of the church will seem less toilsome and complicated. After the long and sometimes complicated day, the pastor will find relief in knowing that a refuge awaits him in the embrace of a loving wife and respectful children. As each new day dawns, this strong support of the family will enable him to face whatever lies in store.

Parsonage life is what the pastor allows it to be. In the final analysis he is responsible for its degree of quality. He can permit intrusions that disrupt the family atmosphere, or he can view and operate the parsonage as the home God intended it to be.

The parsonage is first and foremost the home of the pastor and his family. It is not a youth center, not a communication center, not a church office, nor a Ladies Auxiliary kitchen. It is the one place where the minister and his family should expect to have privacy. For them, it is home. It is the place where the pastor's wife has the right to be an enterprising homemaker, preparing meals which please her family most. It is a house which affords her, within reasonable limits, the opportunity to arrange and decorate according to her own tastes.

A young wife of one pastor was thrilled beyond words while surveying the beauty of her second parsonage. It stood in stark contrast to the wood frame dwelling which was home previously. One influential female member was there to greet the new first family, noticing the wife's excitement over the lovely new home.

The pastor's wife asked, "Will it be alright to decorate and rearrange the furniture?"

A perceptive and wise church member replied, "It is your house now. Arrange it to suit your own tastes."

In another situation a lady was visiting a parsonage one day. After her cursory survey of the parsonage living room, she wryly appraised the surroundings and said, "You know that doilies are out of style now, don't you?"

The pastor's wife replied, "According to my tastes, doilies are never out-of-style."

Point made: end of conversation.

The minister's family should enjoy the parsonage and treat it with care. It is God's gift, His provision. The parsonage as a provision is an Old Testament concept seen in the plan to provide for the Levites. The Levites were the priestly tribe and were consecrated to the service of the Lord's worship. They were not given territorial possessions as were the other tribes. However, they were assigned cities in which to live; and they were allotted land around the cities for their herds and flocks and for the cultivation of their crops and vineyards (Numbers 35:2-5). Thus the concept of providing residence for the man of God continues to be practiced today. Even though the residence is the property of the church, the pastor and his family are free to "be at home," for it is their home while they live there.

Whether it be a parsonage or housing of his own choosing, the pastor's residence is his castle. It is not a prison where the pastor is held against his will in a job he does not like. Neither is it a glass house where he and his family are on constant display to the public. It is a place of comfort and joy where the preacher and his family have a right to normalcy just as much as any lay family. More than just a place to come and go, it is that exclusive conclave which grants tranquility and satisfaction, a place where all the family members may gather around the altar of God for devotion and fellowship, and where they can interact before the Designer of all families who look unto Him for their joys and delights.

REWARDS OF PARENTHOOD

The greatest blessing to any home is the presence of children. If you doubt it, ask the barren woman who has for many years longed to be able to physically give birth to children. If that does not convince you, look to the Word of God, "Lo, children are an heritage of the Lord: and the fruit of the womb is his reward" (Psalm 127:3). In this context, having children is comparable to receiving a rightful inheritance. As with any inheritance, children can turn out to be a blessing or a curse, depending upon the type of development. Along with the blessing comes the awesome responsibility of bringing children up in the nurture and admonition of the Lord.

It was St. Augustine who believed that permanent personality and value development in individuals began at birth. Most certainly his belief was based on the scriptural premise, "Train up a child in the way he should go: and when he is old, he will not depart from it" (Proverbs 22:6). There are very few, if any, who would disagree with this; however, some are made to wonder when children go wrong after efforts have been made to raise them properly. Numbers of ministers with erring children have said, "I did my best. Where did I go wrong?"

When attempting to answer this searching question, the temptation is to ask in return, "Was the best really done for the child?" Children need something other than just admonition from their parents. They learn more by example than from precept. Therefore, parents should build emotionally healthy children through sound advice and godly example.

All parents, laymen and ministers, need to devote much time to being with their children. One pastor wondered why he became estranged from his son until he heard his son complain, "He spends more time with the church than with me. So, I guess he loves the church more than he loves me."

On the other hand, another pastor told me how he went

about being a real father to his only son. First in importance was the obligation to teach him to love the Lord and follow in His ways. Then he devoted some time each day to teach his son how to fish and play ball. The preacher shared a lot of time with his son until the day he left home for college. His son applied himself well in college and in graduate school and, today, that son is an outstanding Christian, a devoted father, a faithful Church of God member, and a successful doctor. The picture might be different today had the father not kept his promise to be faithful to the needs of his son.

Bob Lilley, the former all-pro lineman for the Dallas Cowboys told how he owed so much to his father. Although burdened by a physical handicap, his father instilled in Bob the determination to win and be his best. His father was always there to encourage him and to do whatever he could to help. Today, Bob Lilley is retired from the game of football, but he is considered the greatest Dallas Cowboy defensive lineman of all time. Recently, he was inducted into the pro football hall of fame in Canton, Ohio. I see a significant moral in this story. Though weak or strong, any father, who sees the need for teaching his children, and will do so, will reap lasting results.

Ministers are required to place a great deal of importance on the needs of the church family, and dutifully so. However, in regard to personal and family values, care must be taken to establish proper priorities. The original unit in the Biblical setting is the family. The family remains ahead of the mystical church in importance and even farther ahead of the organized church. Do not fear. When God is made head of all things, all relationships will be maintained and kept in balance. Sons will be taught, daughters will be saved, and the church will continue to grow because of this priority.

With the pressure of the times weighing heavily upon young people, ministers' children should not have to tow the line any more than the average child. Preachers' children are not freaks. They are created by the same God who created the members' children. Yes, they *are* expected to lead Christian lives, but so are laymen's children. Tragically, some preachers militantly demand more from their offspring solely because of an obsession to safeguard their own reputations. The minister should do his best for his children but he certainly ought not expect more of them than does God.

The paramount worry for the minister/father is earning the respect of his children both in and out of the church. Even with the greatest exertion of love and guidance, however, some children still grow up to break the hearts of their parents. It is with great urgency that every minister know how to relate to his children during all phases of their lives. One key way for doing this is through daily interaction.

Every child, especially by the time he is a teenager, has many distractions which vie for attention. It is the home which still has potential for the most powerful direction to personality formation. Dr. Ross Campbell in his book, *How to Really Love Your Teenager* says, "Regardless of the many distractions in the life of a teenager, the home has the deepest influence on his life." The determining factors for either positive or negative influences are the attitudes and actions of the parents.

The types of actions and attitudes are especially important in the area of discipline. Without exception the most significant governing factor is love. Throughout the life of each child, no discipline should be meted out in a vindictive spirit. Even when corporal discipline is necessary, love must be the rule. One minister had to administer such discipline on his son. His son told him afterwards, "You are still the greatest dad in the whole world." Obviously, that son had seen and felt the love of his dad.

If God cares enough to bless any home with children, then He expects the head of that household to provide for all their needs. The psalmist tells us, "Children are an heritage of the Lord" (Psalm 127:3). The child that God gives is an expression of God's favor. Care is the favor parents give back to the child. Care includes providing for emotional, physical, psychological, social and spiritual needs, though not necessarily in that order.

An often-neglected need is the social aspect of a child's life. Children are social creatures who need the fellowship of their peers. The minister should be glad if his children have social advantages. This writer did not have the opportunity to play little league baseball or football. Therefore, it is a joy to be able to live my life over through my only son. I have enjoyed working with him since the day he was big enough to pick up a ball and bat. He has played organized ball for six years now. It is a joy to see him accepted as a person, friend, and fellow-athlete on his teams. It is even more gratifying to know that he is able to fit into society, having been disciplined in all areas of his life.

Our daughter is no exception. She is revealing a love for music and writing. My wife and I swell with pride when she is chosen for a solo part, or when her poetry is chosen for publication in the local newspaper. These things have really happened!

When I pause to reflect on how we have been blessed with respectful children, I have to thank God for the parsonage environment our children have been around. They have been able to do and to see more than the average child simply because they are preacher's kids. I have no worries about their futures. They have experienced love and will have the opportunity to spread the same. We continue to enjoy great times together. We go to church together, eat together, pray together, have devotions together and we plan to go to heaven together.

I stood in line at a fast food restaurant one morning beside a big, muscular gentleman. In front was his little son, dwarfed by this mountain of a man. While they were waiting to be served, the little boy turned around and, looking high up into his dad's face, he said, "I love you, Daddy." Instantly, the man's big hairy arms wrapped around the little boy in loving emotional response.

This *should* be the rule in every parent-child relationship— unabashed expressions of love. Sadly though, we have to accept some harsh and less pleasing realities.

Perhaps you've heard the story of a man who spent much of his son's life doing his own thing and going his own way. Each time his son wanted some time with him, the reply was, "We'll do it tomorrow." Tomorrow never came. Finally, the son grew up and moved away. One day his father called. He asked when his son was coming to see him. The son replied in so many words, that he was too busy. He had no time.

I see another moral here: where no love is given, no love will be returned.

Which do we desire? Do we want our children to be whole persons who know love? Or, do we want them to be victims of chance? Some of the greatest Biblical characters apparently failed as fathers. Because of their failure, sorrow was multiplied through their children.

It has been said that of those listed in *Who's Who,* more are the sons and daughters of ministers than of any other profession. The challenge for ministers to continue teaching the values of industry, integrity, and honesty to their children still exists. The parsonage is more than a dwelling place. It is the base of operation for parental success. Happy is the man who knows this basic fundamental of parenthood, the joy of ministry to his own sons and daughters.

COMFORT OF FAMILY LIFE

Some years ago I read a book entitled *Alive.* This was a true and vivid account of how members of an Uruguayan rugby team survived a plane crash in the Andes mountains. Most who survived the initial impact of the crash survived the entire ordeal which lasted several months before rescue. One great key to their survival was their ability to maintain discipline in the face of overwhelming odds. Evidence of their discipline was revealed in the willingness of each man to do an assigned task cooperatively and without hesitation.

A correlation can be drawn about the minister's family. Where there is cooperation and consideration, a home environment will take on an enjoyable, pleasant atmosphere. When the routine is very demanding, cooperation is absolutely essential. For instance, in most church-goers' homes on Sunday morning, the scene is chaos if there is no cooperation among family members. Picture a family of six or eight with only one bathroom. Need I say more?

Because of this added responsibility on Sundays, the minister and his family must rely on teamwork. The minister is an early riser who should be up before most people, getting everything set for the church service. Since there can be no delays on this all important morning, any given Sunday has explosive potential. On the other hand, of all days in the week, this should be the most peaceful and serene for the minister and his family.

In order to have a good day for himself and his church, the minister should plan every detail. Allow enough time for all activities which are preliminary to the Sunday school and worship hours. Do not permit the enemy to destroy your day before it gets started. Since every minister desires to be a blessing on Sunday morning, it seems only natural he should first bless his family by his presence and his availability to share the demands of preparation.

One minister demanded that his wife and children wait on him hand-and-foot on Sundays. Another minister complained about being late for church because the wife did not have the children ready on time. Neither of these ministers had learned the joy of cooperation, at least on this particular day.

Not one family member need suffer on Sunday, or any other day, if there is true cooperation and consideration. The family which works together in the parsonage will find a reward in the worship service. Joy comes by gaining a victory over potential friction and antagonism. The wife and children should most definitely assist the father/pastor in the most important day of his week. On the other hand, he should consider that this is their day also. If he shows his love and support to his family by assisting in their chores and preparations, God is bound to show favor to him when he ministers to those of his congregation.

Truly, the load shared is more easily carried. This applies also to the emotional and mental loads of various family members. Where a family contains teenagers or pre-teens, the problems become more complex. The pastor who takes time to know his children and who acquaints himself with their schedules and activities will know the joy of being prepared when problems *do* arise in their lives. The pastor/father is a counselor to his children. If he is to be successful in his role, his children need to see him as an example of trust, consistency, and confidence.

Children are influenced most positively by a lifestyle of integrity. What goes on in the home, before the eyes of children, will help shape their own relationships with other people. Therefore, it is vital for the pastor to live consistently before his children. If he preaches to his congregation that families should have devotions and he fails to lead his own family, he has sinned on two counts. If he shows himself unaffectionate to his wife, while giving attention to female members of the congregation, he may not be trusted by his own children as one genuinely concerned.

In regard to his family, the minister must also be a leader in communication. Joy in communication comes when all family members are able to share freely their hurts and animosities with each other. Children long to "let it all hang out," but the foundation for sharing is laid long before by the establishment of a comfortable atmosphere for sharing. Most people—children and adults—are comfortable when they know those who are listening are truly sincere and compassionate. Listening is not done with ears only. The careful observer knows it is done with the heart, the mind, and the eyes. It can be done in most activity settings by the person who genuinely cares and is honest in his approach.

Whether we like to admit it or not, we adults are very transparent in the eyes of young people. They are experts at sensing and tagging phonies. We must show them hearts of love and sincerity.

As a parent with two energetic teenagers, I speak as one who generally understands the cry of a young heart. Attention is being sought, and the right kind of attention at that. Matters which may not seem important to me now, but which were once important to me as a young person, are now items of urgency for my children. Joy comes when we recognize the need right before us in the lives of our children, and when we exert every energy to listen and to act with care.

THE SATISFACTION OF GROWTH AND MATURITY

What a thrill I felt the evening I stood in front of an altar watching my wife-to-be come slowly down the aisle to join me in holy matrimony! My thoughts were many but a poignant idea was, "Soon, she will be bone of my bone and flesh of my flesh."

To this union were born two wonderful offspring. I was thrilled again and again when I saw each for the first time. I will never forget my joy when I saw their ruddy and puffy faces. They had discovered this world well and whole. In my heart, as I thanked God for giving them to me, I thought again, "These are bone of my bone and flesh of my flesh."

Together, we four have carved our unique trail in life and

in the work of the Lord. The parsonage has been that place where we have grown together in spiritual graces.

Surely, the key word for our family life is "together." There have been many times that we four have not been together in the physical realm; but, in terms of purpose and mission, we have been inseparable. The work of the Lord is our life and passion. Where the Lord has bid me go, my wife and children have said "yes" to God also. They have shared my joys and tears. The ministry has taken us to a variety of places, and confronted us with different people and problems; but, in every place and circumstance, our togetherness has been a source of mutual strength.

Our accommodations have ranged from a one-room dwelling to a spacious two-story brick parsonage with an abundance of bedrooms and bathrooms. God has always provided. But regardless of the physical dwelling place, the actual home has been wherever we have been together. Thanks be to God for all the joys of the parsonage.

Through various stages of discouragement and triumph my faithful wife and children have been by my side. They have shared in everything. The same is true in all parsonages where genuine love, concern and cooperation exist. I do not claim to be a perfect father or minister, neither do I claim to have a perfect home or family. There have been times of disappointment and disagreement, but we have overcome all difficulties through prayer and consideration for each other.

As I look back upon our years together, they have moved along very rapidly. Soon our two teenage children will be away from the protective umbrella of the minister's home, fending for themselves. That will be a sad day; yet it will be a glad day. It will be sad to see them leave our environment, but it will be a joy knowing that the strength of parsonage life will go with them. It is my firm belief that ministers' children have more going for them than just about anyone else. Thus I rejoice.

From my own experience, I can say my family and I have found joy in the parsonage. It has provided a stability which has enabled us to summon strength to face and surmount all problems. On many occasions Satan has come against our children, but he hasn't won. Our children are acquainted with Jesus also. They know how to call on Him. I realize that I am not alone in this. Many other ministers know the joy of spiritual growth and maturity in each family member. This maturity in the family brings support to the minister in and out of the parsonage. If there is to be a successful ministry, this aspect of joy must remain. This formula for success will lead to happiness and peace for any family that occupies the parsonage.

CONCLUSION

I was in a certain home some years ago. The house was of modest decor and design. On the wall hung a simple plaque which stood out like the blazing sun. It read, "Christ is the head of this house."

Unequivocally, I accept this as the basis for success and happiness in any home, including the parsonage. Where there is joy in the parsonage, Jesus is always the center of attention. If this fundamental remains intact, we can expect ministers and their ministries to be more fruitful and effective in days ahead.

Potentially, the parsonage holds a faith and confidence which can be found no place else. The parsonage is not utopia but it is a place where all family members do not worry about fighting demons and devils. It is a place where the minister and his family have the edge in the battle against Satan. It is a place where true reliance upon God can bring about the experience of successful parenthood. The parsonage should be filled with the healing presence of the Lord. With that presence, every minister's family has the potential to be well and whole in every respect.

3

THE OUTSIDE WORLD

B. Paul Jones

In contrast to home environment and intimate personal relations, the pastor is privileged and challenged to rub shoulders almost on a daily basis with men and women of every type and caliber. The genuinely called man of God sees this as something good, not as a burden. He learns to cultivate these contacts, to turn that which is normally thought of as social, perhaps a drudgery, into something spiritual and enjoyable. In brief, whether it be fellowship with a businessman in the city, luncheon with a banker, fishing with a friend, or a coffee break with a drop-in visitor, a minister's contact with this outside world can become a fertile field for ministry and a chief source of joy.

COMMUNITY CONTACTS

The minister is a professional person, expected to associate with others. He is to assume a fair share of community responsibilities. Many requests will be made to the pastor for cooperation with other ministers in charitable and educational activities. He must select with care those organizations to which he can give valuable time. Some enterprises deserve support in order that the pastor may refer certain needy cases to them. A well established city mission is an example of one such charitable work.

There are several other areas where the minister can exert a positive influence for furthering educational activities. Many members of the church are active in Parent-Teacher Associations. The pastor can attend these group meetings and give support to many of their activities. He should visit the schools whenever he has the opportunity. He can offer help to the principals and superintendents of schools in his area. Generally, such professional people will appreciate the pastor's interest and they may call upon him for special projects with other ministers or for suggestions regarding school problems.

By these type of involvements, one is recognizing that a minister is a leader to many beyond his own church and denomination. When properly handled and kept in perspective, this can be and should be a source of joy to the pastor.

On one occasion I was called upon to render community service by dedicating a factory building. Years earlier a dear brother in my church had started a business in the basement of his home. The business outgrew his basement, moved into one factory, and a short time later into an even more spacious factory building, soon employing a large number of workers, many of whom were Christians.Through the years the man sought the blessings of God upon his efforts and his business was increasing substantially. He had secured government contracts. Many other new accounts were being added. I was called upon to preside at the dedication for the employees and the new and larger facilities.

I could readily observe how grateful this brother was. As I joined in the guided tour and met many of his customers and officers from various other companies, many employees seemed influenced in a positive manner and, once again, I experienced the joy of ministry through extending the message of Christ into the everyday work place.

BUSINESS CONTACTS

Jesus said a great deal about sowing seed, gathering harvests, leavening meal. He spoke of shining lights and new wine. All of which points to the importance of the expansion of His kingdom. His teachings reveal Christ expects His kingdom to grow. As ministers of God we have responsibility to testify with integrity.

It has been my privilege during my pastorates to become involved in several building and expansion programs. These have provided special contacts with attorneys, bank officials, architects, city officials and inspectors, as well as many building contractors. Such business contacts have afforded me the opportunity to represent Christ and His church in a very unique manner.

During the course of erecting a new church, several people who were connnected with building responsibilities attended our services for their first time. As a result, some have become regular attenders of our church. One such man, a mechanical engineer, became so interested and involved with our building program that he donated his entire fee which amounted to several thousands of dollars. And to this day he continues to be a very fine Christian professional.

While I do not take personal credit for this accomplishment, I do feel strongly that it is important to represent what we do as a spiritual work and to demonstrate how a new church can serve the community. I cannot overemphasize the importance of representing our spiritual labors to all business and professional people we contact. Any minister will feel a deep sense of joy and satisfaction as he fulfills his high calling within the business world. When his spiritual work is observed by the business and professional society, it is then that the pastor receives the recognition and support his church deserves in the community.

Most business leaders judge the entire membership by the way a pastor is seen in the community. If this image is positive, then the witnessing power of the Lord Jesus Christ in the world has been enhanced. Surely there is no greater joy for any pastor than to know he is carrying out the Great Commission of Jesus Christ.

A number of scriptural passages undergird this idea that the pastor must hold forth the church's integrity to the business world. Solomon wrote, "Seest thou a man diligent in his business? He shall stand before kings . . ." (Proverbs 22:29). And Paul told us to be, "Not slothful in business; fervent in spirit; serving the Lord" (Romans 12:11).

SOCIAL CONTACTS

Jesus said, "Ye are the salt of the earth; but if the salt have lost his savour, wherewith shall it be salted? it is thenceforth good for nothing, but to be cast out, and to be trodden under foot of men" (Matthew 5:13).

As we penetrate into the world and associate with its people, agencies, and institutions, we soon realize how powerfully and constantly we serve as salt. Salt dissolves and disappears when it is best serving its purpose. It is useless so long as it retains its identity in the saltshaker. Salt is always expendable. And Jesus said, "Ye are the salt of the earth."

Jesus also said, "Ye are the light of the world. A city that is set on a hill cannot be hid" (Matthew 5:14). Light does not exist for its own sake, but to illuminate everything else. We are most conscious of light when it is dark. We are least aware of it when it illuminates properly. "Ye are the light of the world."

Ministry is not confined to the inside of the church only. It belongs to the work place, to offices, factories, farms, schools and to wherever the Christian has a contact point with the world. We are called to a sacred vocation of missionary, evangelist, witness, commanded and empowered to be the salt of the earth, the light of the world. "Let your light so shine before men, that they may see your good works, and glorify your Father which is in heaven" (Matthew 5:16).

The pastor who involves himself in social activities must not forget the scrutiny of watching eyes. He is to be a living, positive advertisement for the transforming power of Christ. He must keep in contact with the world but must not permit his life to be fashioned by the pattern of the world.

Although our high calling under God and our freedom within the boundaries of His Word will sometimes separate us from certain social activities, the pastor should keep the same purpose in mind which was evident in the Lord's attendance of social activities. God's glory should be the goal. Then we will derive a great sense of fulfillment in sharing a Christ-like testimony.

The story is told of a missionary who approached a town with the Gospel for what he thought was the first time. After telling of God sending His Son to love men and to die for them, the people responded, "We already know him. He came to us, lived among us, and died here."

The missionary was surprised. He repeated the story of Jesus. Again the people responded "We know him."

Finally, the missionary pieced together the news of a former missionary who had been so like Christ that the people actually confused him with his Savior. Thus, we too show the life of Christ to the world by the way we live each day. "Thou wilt shew me the path of life: in thy presence is fulness of joy; at thy right hand there are pleasures for evermore" (Psalm 16:11).

RECREATIONAL CONTACTS

In the early years of my pastorate, I became acquainted with several men through contacts at the local YMCA. Little did I realize at the time that I would soon need the services of these professional men in our church expansion program. There were realtors, attorneys, tax consultants, brokers, and insurance men. Needless to say, this young pastor came to realize that God certainly did know his needs. From those casual contacts there developed areas of communications which assisted me greatly in the work of the Lord.

I remember especially one gentleman who had no relationship with Christ or the church. I was the only minister he had known. Whatever else he might have thought of me, he soon found out I wasn't abnormal. He confided in me during those relaxed times and said to me at a later date, "I don't know what I would have done without having you to talk to during these troubled times." By some miracle his marriage was saved and also his business.

Such casual and recreational contacts with the outside world can be very productive for the cause of Christ and they increase one's faith in the life-changing power of the Word of God.

INTER-DENOMINATIONAL CONTACTS

Jesus said, ". . . but whosoever will be great among you, let him be your minister; and whosoever will be chief among you, let him be your servant; even as the Son of Man came not to be ministered unto, but to minister, and to give his life a ransom for many" (Matthew 20:26-28).

There is a sense in which a pastor is a servant of servants. He must never forget that night when the Lord girded

Himself with a towel and washed the disciples' feet. Neither must the pastor forget that he is called to serve Christ.

We must determine what our Lord would actually do if He were still on earth. We must discover how the mind of Christ would work in order that we as ministers might follow Him in our everyday life. Paul said in Philippians, "Let this mind be in you, which was also in Christ Jesus: Who, being in the form of God . . . made himself of no reputation, and took upon him the form of a servant . . . , And being found in fashion as a man, he humbled himself, and became obedient unto death, even the death of the cross" (Philippians 2:5-8).

To think like Christ then is to seek what is best for others. That was His example when He took the place of a servant and did what the disciples were at first unwilling to do. His own words were being fulfilled—"But the Son of Man came to minister . . ."—and we also can minister to one another through everyday contacts with peers and fellow workers.

"I have to go to a committee meeting! There are so many other places I would prefer to go. I wish I did not have to attend."

Do those statements sound familiar?

Committee work need not be boring nor should it be a waste of time. It can be a spiritual tonic, a time looked to with pleasure and joy. Judging by the number of committee meetings that are held in any denomination, they are certainly a vital necessity. Knowing that a committee meeting is called, we should remember to ask the Lord for His blessings on His work, and for wisdom to make right decisions. However well we may be acquainted with the matter at hand, we need guidance beyond our own to do the work of the Lord efficiently and effectively.

A number of committee chairmen come to mind who made their meetings a time for worship as well as for business. This gave a spiritual tone to the discussions. Each member of the committee would make it his aim to promote Christian fellowship. The warmth of this fellowship would strengthen each one in his determination to serve the Lord to the best of his ability. When we are enthusiastic for our own views, it is easy to put them forward even to the exclusion of contrary views. We should remember the words of James, "My beloved brethren, let every man be swift to hear, slow to speak, slow to wrath" (James 1:19). This will help promote joyful fellowship even in tough situations.

It is good to remind ourselves of the real object of our meeting together. It is the Lord's work and not ours that we are trying to do. This thought urges us to remember it is God's glory we are seeking. No matter what other success we may obtain, failure to seek God's will is complete failure. Jesus Christ must be at the center of all we do in His name. When we seek the glory of God in committee work, we shall find it not drudgery but a means of spiritual growth. I have accepted committee assignments because I sincerely felt it was God's call to me. I look upon it as an opportunity for joyful service for the Master. Inter-denominational as well as denominational committee meetings can serve for spiritual growth to any minister.

DENOMINATIONAL CONTACTS

The minister can find ministerial meetings a helpful source of inspiration. I look forward to those special times where my peers gather for prayer and intercession, or for study and examination of Scriptures. As members of the Body of Christ we find such meetings to be rich in fellowship. Other meetings also provide means and ways by which the Body may be edified. The instructions provided by leaders are valuable to every minister. Paul stated to Timothy, "Till I come, give attendance to reading, to exhortation, to doctrine. Neglect not the gift that is in thee, which was given thee by prophecy, with the laying on of the hands of the presbytery. Meditate upon these things; give thyself wholly to them; that thy profiting may appear to all" (1 Timothy 4:13-15).

My early days of ministry were wonderfully influenced by the power of the Holy Spirit demonstrated at these times of gathering together. Healings, miracles, and the operation of other gifts of the Spirit made a lasting impression upon me.

Not all, but most ministers work in close proximity with others on district or state levels. Such provides extraordinary opportunity for fellowship and recreation that can light up one's life. There is great profit in these times of meeting, when we hear from each other and from the Holy Spirit as to our call in the Lord. These moments can serve as times of encouragement and refreshment. We are reminded of our mission in the ministry and of the joy that is promised by Christ: "These things have I spoken unto you, that my joy might remain in you, and that your joy might be full" (John 15:11). "And the ransomed of the Lord shall return, and come to Zion with songs and everlasting joy upon their heads" (Isaiah 35:10).

PASTORAL CONTACTS

We often call it soul-winning. That is precisely what hospital visitation can result in for the dedicated minister. Perhaps no other facet in all the ministry can be more fruitful in reaching the outside world for Christ. While my task is normally in the realm of providing spiritual guidance and comfort to the member patient, it often leads into an introduction to new acquaintances. These new people are attracted to the Gospel through an invitation from me to listen while I read the Scriptures and pray for the member with whom they are sharing the room. With a cheerful, optimistic, and positive approach, one can make a lifetime impression upon the individual for the ministry of the church.

I recall an incident while visiting a member of our church who suffered with terminal cancer. Although the hospital was located across the city, I managed to visit three or four times a week. During this two months' time, there were several patients in and out, sharing this room. It was my privilege to be a witness to them. By my regular visiting, reading the Bible and praying, numerous questions would arise from them and I was able to minister on a personal basis. More than one came to visit our church. One of these men and his entire family became members of our church. The man told me later, "I observed the love of Christ as you would come into our room for a visit and I found myself looking forward to your visit more than to my physician. That's when I was convinced my spiritual need was greater than I had realized."

One cannot amply express the joy and keen satisfaction experienced by such events as these. Yet this is the promise of God if we will follow Him: "He that goeth forth and weepeth, bearing precious seed, shall doubtless come again with rejoicing, bringing his sheaves with him" (Psalm 126:6).

On another occasion, while visiting a child who was a regular rider on the church bus, I entered his hospital room and, standing near the entrance door, paused. His mother was by his bedside and he said, "Look mother! There's Jesus!" Needless to say, this had to be the greatest compliment I could ever hope to receive as a minister, even though it was given by a little child. This dear family also became members of our church later on.

One never knows the positive influence rendered for Christ and the church when he approaches hospital contacts in a spiritual nature. The joy of ministry is never more realized than when I see people become more spiritually minded and conscious of their needs. It is in this setting, although outside the walls of the church building, where the claims of Christ can be presented in a very successful manner.

This type of contact with the outside world re-enforces the fact that Christianity is not a private spiritual luxury, not something to be kept apart from daily life, but it is a living force to be applied to all areas of life. This is what the minister's calling in life is all about. Whether we are aware of it or not, the persons observing us are forming an opinion as to what we are. Our life in the public world, and their opinion of us, is predicated upon what people perceive us to be. Generally speaking, people are drawn to to a warm, outgoing, positive personality. They tend to be "turned off" by a gloomy disposition and negative attitudes. So God is wanting ministers who have the ability to shine for Him, who are themselves completely sold on the Gospel, and who present that gospel wherever they go. Sometimes we may not even consciously do this; but, by the vibrations other people receive from us, by our compassion for them, they pick up on the message of love and concern.

God truly wants us to be His genuine, joyful ambassadors in the world.

The funeral service is another contact by the pastor which takes place more and more outside the church. While the funeral service of the unsaved will be one of the most difficult services the minister will have to conduct, it is a wonderful opportunity to provide help to people who are in need, and to bring the blessing of faith. A contact in the home of the bereaved can be constructive and consoling. It is likely that certain relatives and friends of the deceased will consider their own spiritual condition in the light of this loss. This is a good time to display practical Christian love. When entering and leaving this new home, a sympathetic attitude and a spirit of hope will surely be noticed by the outside world.

I have always endeavored to mention some good done in the unsaved person's lifetime, but I raise no false hopes regarding eternal destiny. I feel the funeral is not the time for extemporaneous preaching, but the message should be designed to help and comfort the living. A follow-up visit to the home of the bereaved family a few days after the funeral will reap great benefits for the kingdom of God. It is times like these where the church's ministry enjoys its finest hour. By being there in time of need and by being willing to give of yourself in service to the unsaved you bring added dimensions to your ministry.

WEEKLY CONTACTS

It is impossible to enumerate all the contacts a pastor may make during any given week. In addition to office encounters, he may visit the nursing home where the elderly are in need. He may travel the hospital corridors to visit those of all ages who are terminally ill. He is on call at all hours to give comfort to the bereaved. He may move on to another hospital where he rejoices over a successful operation or the birth of a baby. He occasionally struggles with suicidal people, trying to give them a reason to live. He agonizes with alcoholics in their private hell of addiction. He tries to comfort spouses during broken relationships. He prays with distraught mothers and fathers whose children are going wrong. He will often deal with the man or woman who comes into his office from off the street.

Interruptions, emergencies and crises are all part of any pastor's week. These are really the reasons for our calling. We want to be used of God in leading people toward spiritual maturity. We want to reveal the joys of Christ even in difficult situations.

At the mention of joyful Christian service, some people say, "It is all right for you to talk that way, but I feel differently." I have this question. Does Christ's promise of joy depend on circumstances? How could it? Think of the setting in which most of the Bible was written. Persecution, trials, imprisonment—those early Christians had it rough. Yet their joyous note rings down through the centuries.

So the joy of Christian service which Jesus offers to us is not conditional on what happens in our lives. Even the anticipation of joy can affect us positively.

The joy of winning keeps the athlete driving his body in pain. The joy of achieving good grades motivates the student to diligent study. The joy of being reunited with family and friends keeps us driving long distances. Note the words in Hebrews: ". . . Jesus, the author and finisher of our faith; who, for the joy that was set before him endured the cross, despising the shame . . ." (Hebrews 12:2). Joy in the service of the King—that makes all things bearable.

Please know that I am a pastor because I want to be in service for my Lord. The joy and satisfaction of ministry far outweigh whatever burdens or trials may have to be endured.

CONCLUSION

The seventy were chosen and set apart by Jesus to aid Him in His glorious service (Luke 10:1, 9). They were to be the heralds of God's Kingdom. If men received them, they were to rejoice. They experienced such great success that their hearts overflowed with praise. They came back to Jesus full of joy.

A thrill awaits you when you become a witness and carry the word of life. You will receive far more than you can realize. You will make new friends, find new fellowship, and enter into countless other joys. Jesus Christ enjoyed His contact with people: so will you in His name.

The concern for winning multitudes through television and radio has caused many to lose sight of the individual. Christ never lost sight of the significance of ministry to one individual. Surely He enjoyed being with people, since He ate with Zacchaeus and Matthew. Of Jesus it was said, "He ate with sinners." On one occasion, Jesus was treated with such appreciation that a woman who had been forgiven washed His feet and dried them with her hair.

Our Lord's ministry was not limited to the inside of the

synagogue on the Sabbath day. He made contact with people by a dusty road (John 7:37), at the city well (John 4:13), near the seashore (Luke 8:27), at the table of a host (Luke 7:44), at death's door (Luke 8:49), and outside the city gates (John 4:30). Jesus was always open to people.

So many people in today's world have troubles and torment. Few of us know the miseries and difficulties which hide behind an otherwise pleasant countenance. It is a great tragedy that so few people really care. Most are too busy with business, entertainment, and self-interest to sympathize long with those in need.

Think what it must have meant to lepers to have a friendly, warm hand touch their untouchable bodies! No wonder children swarmed about Christ! They loved His sympathetic touch. As Christ's ministry was, so is ours to be in their world (1 John 4:17). As we lift the burdened heart, comfort a bereaved soul, or bring good news of salvation, we are blessing others in a manner never to be forgotten. Because of this ministry, we bring joy to others.

For the individual Christian, the secret of joy lies in consciousness of God. We should be joyful because we have been raised from the dead to the promise of an inheritance incorruptible, sure, enduring forever; and because, when trials do come, we are kept by the power of God.

It was the joyfulness of the early Christians which attracted the non-Christian world. Ample evidence of this is found in the beginnings of Christianity at Rome. The Roman citizen knew how to suffer nobly. He saw this often, and he endured with a grim patience, but his heart never bubbled with such joy and ecstasy as demonstrated by the early Christians. The first manifestation of conversion which the Roman witnessed in his neighbor was a radiant joyousness. This Christian joy is also a fruit of the Spirit. It is not dependent on external conditions, but upon internal possessions such as grace, divine power, and uninterrupted fellowship with the Lord. It depends upon companionship with Jesus Christ, and the infilling of the Holy Spirit. This joy is far more than mere happiness. Happiness fluctuates. It is influenced by circumstances, by external conditions, but genuine Christian joy increases under trials. It abounds wherever Christ abides. Paul and Silas knew what joy meant, and what it did for them in the Philippian jail.

The things which Jesus had spoken of to His disciples should be the productive source of their joy. What a joy to be redeemed from sin! What a joy to be adopted into the family of God! What a joy to be in harmony with God, and to walk in the path of Christian duty! What a joy to have our interests linked with the interests of God, to have the words of Christ producing in us a joy unspeakable and full of glory. This kind of joy will always translate into contended service for our Lord.

4

THE PRIVATE PLACE

Hoyt E. Stone

INTRODUCTION

Probably the best description of a minister is found in the word servant. Jesus used this term when he noted that whoever would be greatest in the Kingdom of heaven should be servant to all (Matthew 23:11). He lived out this point by becoming a servant Himself, as witness not only His deeds but the meaning of his actions the night he washed the disciples' feet (John 13:2-17). Servanthood is not a trait natural to fallen man. It comes only through God's grace and a transformed life. Nevertheless, it is possible to live such a life and the minister must constantly strive to do so.

Few things more dramatically point up this servant role than the ministry of counseling, or the minister's role as advisor to people needing help. We have chosen to refer to counseling ministry as "the private place" primarily in order to emphasize the confidential nature of this work.

The minister has always been viewed as a servant of society. In colonial America it was the minister who taught children to read, the minister who always participated in political and social decisions, the minister who normally became spokesman or ambassador for the community. While today, other professionals share this community or social responsibility, such as lawyers, teachers, specialists of all types, it nevertheless remains true that ministers are often seen as sources of advice and information, especially by certain segments of the community.

Every minister must recognize this fact and he must be prepared to function in an advisory capacity. Though some do more of this type of work than others, there is no way to avoid it totally, even if the minister were so inclined.

Wayne Oates wrote in, *An Introduction to Pastoral Counseling* (Nashville, Broadman, 1959):

> The pastor, regardless of his training, does not enjoy the privilege of electing whether or not he will counsel with his people. They inevitably bring their problems to him for his best guidance and wisest care. He cannot avoid this if he stays in the pastoral ministry. His choice is not between counseling or not counseling, but between counseling in a disciplined and skilled way and counseling in an undisciplined and unskilled way.

Admittedly, there are some dangers in this type of ministry today, some pitfalls and snares rather unknown a generation back. Ministers now run the risk of being sued for poor advice or for the wrong advice.

In 1979 Kenneth Mark Nally, age 24, shot himself to death. His troubled parents blamed their son's suicide on the church, claiming that the pastors counseled their son that suicide was an acceptable alternative to a life of sin. A California appeals court ruled that a jury should decide if the church and its ministers were guilty of clergy malpractice.

An Oklahoma court awarded $390,000 to a woman who said her church had caused her emotional distress when it branded her a fornicator.

A California jury awarded $2.1 million to a Santa Clara woman who said the church defrauded her by failing to fulfill promises to improve her life.

The Supreme Court has declared that the interest of the state in protecting a child's life overrides parents' religious rights to refuse medical care for the child. This is our world today.

Some would claim that churches and lawyers are more vulnerable to lawsuits today because they are stretching their helping hands out of the sanctuary and into the streets. Churches now provide day care for children, soup kitchens for the hungry, and clothes for the needy. They give haven for refugees, beds to the homeless, and counseling to the confused. The truth is, though, that the church has always done such things. What has changed is the attitude of people in a materialistic world. People today have a heightened sense of personal importance if not greed. They feel someone ought to pay for their misery, and they will sue for just about anything.

However, the watchword for the minister must be "caution," not "cowardice." God's men must not back away from the task. They must not let up on the church's historical commitments nor hesitate to fulfill the Lord's commission.

PEOPLE NEED AND ARE LOOKING FOR SANCTUARY

Life never takes place in a vacuum. It is seldom calm. People hurt. They are in pain. Often that pain is written on their faces or it is seen in the blankness of their eyes. Drugs mute the pain but do not truly heal. Alcohol dulls the senses but it offers no real solution. In this pain and out of this suffering more people than ever are looking for sanctuary, a private place, a shelter from life's stress and strain. The minister must prove himself a friend. He must become that someone whom people can trust.

It is a mistake for the minister to think he must have a professional counseling degree in order to help people. Even if he does have such a degree, no minister has a resource so powerful or so effective as the gospel of Jesus Christ. The minister is first of all a bearer of good news. That good news boils down to, "God is love. He is reconciling the world unto Himself through Jesus Christ." Such news will help any man, any woman, regardless of circumstances. While counseling may go beyond these simple boundaries, Christian counseling cannot really begin *other* than at this terminus.

Armed with such knowledge of God's saving grace, and strengthened through the power of God's Holy Spirit, the minister has marvelous truths to share. He must learn first to listen and he must then apply the simple truth of the gospel with love and concern, never fearing, but always trusting for God to bring the touch of miracle which changes lives. Herein is joy indeed.

They usually come very hesitantly, feeling the minister out, tentatively reaching like a child for love they are not sure will be there—those lost souls who seek a private place, who wish someone with whom to talk. It takes a sensitive man, it takes a spiritual man to understand their hesitancy and feel the pain, a man who does not rush matters but who encourages and gently leads until a soul is laid bare.

One young man met a pastor at the local service station. He chatted about the weather, about life in the army, finally about his girl friend. He haltingly asked the minister if he might drop by his office some time for a chat. The pastor smiled and urged him on. "Any time."

The young man surprised the pastor a few days later. He sat nervously, squirming from side to side. Was real slow to get to the point. Raised in a Christian home, having served in the Army for four years, he was recently home and truly interested in a young lady from a neighboring town. He had thought the romance going fine. Thought he loved the girl. Now, however, he was troubled. She had invited him to go to bed with her, prior to the wedding. She did not think the way he imagined a girl should think. Did not have the values he wanted in a wife, though she displayed attitudes he and his army pals had sanctioned in Vietnam. Puzzled, troubled, very lonely, the young man needed a friend, someone with whom to talk.

The pastor became that friend, that someone, that bit of sanity and stability in a young man's troubled world. It was not a story to be told, not a victory to be shared by the pastor even with his wife, but it was a secret little triumph between him and the Lord, between him and the young man. It was a victory which brightened the pastor's days then: it is one which still glows warmly, twenty years later. Just one lonely soul and a minister, meeting in a private place, sharing the truths of life and the grace of Jesus Christ—this exemplifies the small things of which the minister's joy is made.

THE MAN OF GOD MUST CULTIVATE THIS COUNSELING MINISTRY

Such does not mean necessarily that the minister will advertise himself as a counselor, though that too is all right if he is trained and if such appeals to him, but the minister must let people know he is available for private interviews, private meetings, private sharing sessions.

Nor may it always be wise for the pastor to announce his counseling ministry from the pulpit, or to solicit clients. Most likely there will be enough of this type work coming naturally. But the minister must prove himself trustworthy. He must guard confidences and protect those who trust him, never hinting or in any way passing this information along, not even to his wife and the parsonage family. Only thus, through absolute confidentiality of the private place, can the pastor build a counseling ministry. Only then will the lonely come seeking his spiritual aid and strength.

Ministry in the private place does not begin full-blown. It is not at once something that falls in a man's lap. Rather, like a garden in spring, it is a ministry which must be cultivated. First, one must plant the seed, then he must water, and patiently wait for the growing season. Eventually he who ministers in the private place will reap a crop that brings great joy and satisfaction to the heart. It comes with time and a growing reputation as servant to others.

Gary Collins reminds us quite accurately in *Christian Counseling* (Waco: Word, 1980) that it is important for counselors to have an understanding of problems (how they arise and how they might be resolved), and a familiarity with counseling skills. But he goes on to point out that recent research seems to indicate that therapeutic techniques can only be potent when the counselor has a personality which is inherently helpful—that is, when the pastor is characterized by warmth, sensitivity, understanding, concern, and a willingness to confront people in an attitude of love.

Dr. Collins further quotes psychologist C. H. Patterson as stating,

> To be most effective the therapist must be a real, human person . . . offering a genuine human relationship . . . Much of what therapists do is superfluous or unrelated to their effectiveness; in fact, it is likely that much of their success is unrelated to what they do or even occurs in spite of what they do, as long as they offer the relationship that it appears therapists of very differing persuasions do provide . . . It is a relationship characterized not so much by what techniques the therapist uses as by what he is, not so much by what he does as by the way he does it.

From such one finds it easy to conclude that every minister who has a calling from God, and who genuinely wishes to be helpful in the servant-relationship spirit of Christ, moves into the private place with marked advantages over the professional who sees but a client. The minister's counseling usually extends beyond the private place, flowing over into daily contacts and even into the philosophy and the theology of his pulpit. In this sense as well, he is blessed and positioned to witness a success which brings joy to the heart.

In fact, every true minister will bring to bear on the counseling ministry the full support of the Christian fellowship which he represents. Jesus said we are to "love one another." Over and again, throughout the New Testament we run into this expression, "one another." We are told to edify and build up one another (Romans 14:19); to be hospitable to one another (Romans 15:7); to instruct or admonish one another (Romans 15:14); to be kindly affectioned one to another and in honor to prefer one another (Romans 12:10); to live peaceably with one another (Romans 12:18); to serve one another in love (Galatians 5:13); to be kind one to another, tenderhearted, forgiving (Ephesians 4:32); to teach and admonish one another in psalms and hymns (Colossians 3:16); to comfort ourselves together and edify one another (1 Thessalonians 5:11); to confess faults one to another and to pray one for another (James 5:16); and to love one another because God is love (1 John 4:7).

In order to cultivate a counseling ministry it goes without saying that the minister should do everything in his power to equip himself well for the task. It will not be possible in this short chapter to discuss thoroughly some of the important ingredients which make for effective counseling but I would like to recommend a specific book, *Christian Counseling: A Comprehensive Guide* by Gary R. Collins, Ph.D. (Waco: Word Books, 1980) and to share from Dr. Collins' introduction to his work three important items.

First, there are noticeable characteristics to be found in those men who are effective counselors. Dr. Collins lists three:

1. *Warmth.* This is the art of caring, respecting, or possessing a sincere, nonsmothering concern for the person who has ventured into the private place.

2. *Genuineness.* The minister must be real—open, sincere, avoiding phoniness or the temptation to play a superior role.

3. *Empathy.* This is not necessarily sympathy but it is the ability to "feel with" another, to actually get into the problem with him or her.

True, all of these may come naturally to the man of God who truly loves people but it seems good to list the individual characteristics and it might be well for the minister as a counselor to examine himself in light of particular incidents just to see how he rates. Does he possess and exemplify these characteristics?

Second, it will help us to look at what Dr. Collins calls the goals of counseling. We mean something more specific than leading a person to Christ, or helping one through a temporary crisis. Counseling goals may be listed as five items.

1. *Self-understanding.* Many people are confused. They have little concept of what they are, where they are going, or what they ought to be doing with their lives. The minister's task in the private place is to help them find the way.

2. *Communication.* Especially in marriage or family problems, people have difficulty talking with one another. They tend to hide their feelings, to ignore the rising bitterness solely because they have either lost or failed to develop the art of communication. In the private place the minister must help them realize the problem, help them understand that it is possible to reach out, to communicate the inner feelings of the soul.

3. *Learning and Behavior Change.* Let us face it: some people have bad habits, behavior patterns which constantly complicate and negate their efforts to establish proper relationships with other people. Only two solutions are available: the minister must either help change all the others, which is not likely, or he must change the one who is before him for help. It must be done quietly, in private, slowly, and in confidence. But it can be done when the minister has a goal in mind. To ignore the need for such change is indeed a dangerous error.

4. *Self-actualization* or as Collins prefers *Christ-Actualization.* It is important for people to learn to develop and achieve their maximum potential. For the Christian minister it is understood that man cannot do this within himself but only through the grace of God. With Christ as Lord and helper, however, hurting men and women can learn to live free of their pain. The minister must teach this truth in the private place. Then comes the joy of ministry.

5. *Support.* There will be some people who come to the

minister so bound and so troubled that they have long since lost the ability to make it on their own. These people need love, they need a listening ear, they need understanding, but they also need support, actual outside help and strength. There is no better agency for this than the Christian fellowship. It is the minister's responsibility to see that such people are introduced to a proper support system before being turned back into the marketplace of life. The minister must find this support for them, either through family, through friends, or through the church itself.

Finally, along with these characteristics of effective counseling and these goals of counseling, let us note a few of the techniques of counseling. Dr. Collins lists these as four: attending, listening, responding, and teaching. Under the third of these, responding, he discusses:

—leading, a skill by which the counselor slightly anticipates the counselee's direction of thought and responds in a way that redirects the conversation.

—reflecting, a way of letting counselees know that we are with them.

—questioning, another method of directing the conversation and one to be used cautiously by the beginning counselor.

—confronting, presenting some idea which the one needing help might not otherwise see, but always done in a loving, caring, non-judgmental way.

—informing, giving facts to those in need of information.

—interpreting, explaining to one what his or her behavior or other events actually mean.

—supporting and encouraging, reassuring the person that you are truly with him or her, and that you will not fade away or betray the confidence.

Thus the minister can and should cultivate and broaden his contacts with people. Through counseling he can hope to help others in the Spirit of Jesus Christ. Once again it is noted, such may not happen immediately: it comes with time and with a growing reputation, as people learn to respect and value the benefits of that private place between minister and parishioner.

IMPORTANCE OF THE PRIVATE PLACE

One understands the importance of the private place—that place where people can talk with the minister in confidence—only when he realizes what the minister represents to the average man or woman. This may not be true in every locality, and there may always be exceptions, but by and large the average American has natural respect and deep appreciation for clergymen and what they represent. You can find few people in this country who are totally devoid of any type religious heritage. Those who are rather skeptical of certain men, or of certain religions, will often still have respect for religion in some form or another. It is important that the minister recognize this fact.

For hurting people, troubled people, distraught people, people in crisis, the minister represents all that is mysterious and yet promising. He is the symbol of faith, the visual representative of God's kingdom on earth, the place where it all comes together whether the seeker fully understands what is involved or not. The minister must go into those private sessions, not with an exaggerated concept of himself and of his own ability, but with full appreciation of what he represents.

There will be days or times when the minister will go into the inner sanctum without feeling very special himself. There will be occasions when he is overwhelmed at the magnitude of the problem, so much so that he will be tempted to despair; but the minister must not lose hope. He must not show weakness. He must not in any way betray what he represents, even though his feelings run totally opposite.

Here is an example. Jessica Smith (not her real name) went to her pastor's office seeking counsel and also desiring prayer for healing. She explained that she had been to three doctors. They had given her conflicting reports. She was troubled, confused, not sure what to do; but she had been praying. She now felt that her only hope was for the pastor to pray for her. She had come for that purpose and desired to be anointed and prayed for, just like the Bible said.

There you have one side of the situation. At the same time, the pastor was suffering from a flu virus. He did not tell Jessica he was sick—what possible benefit would that have been?—but he dutifully dressed and kept the appointment just as a minister is supposed to do. Here was a lady seeking help for her physical affliction: here was a man of God suffering also from physical illness.

Were they to despair together? Was the minister to forget his duty? What he represented? His commission to heal the sick? Of course not!

What the pastor did on this occasion was encourage the faith he saw in Jessica. He first sent her into the church sanctuary to kneel at the altar and pray. He strengthened his own faith through a moment of private devotion, remembering he was God's servant, called and anointed to serve whether he felt healthy or sick. He then walked into the sanctuary himself, anointed Jessica in the name of Jesus Christ, and prayed for her healing.

Jessica went home. That very afternoon she called the parsonage, rejoicing. God had healed her completely.

The minister can never afford to forget what he represents. The private place is something important to many people and the minister must capitalize on that faith and confidence in God.

The importance of the private place is further highlighted in that it is here where the pastor meets people under such varied circumstances. All of us have a natural tendency to hide our true feelings. The minister cannot look in the faces of a Sunday morning congregation and know for sure how folks are feeling. There is a mask over the faces. The heart is known only to the Spirit of God. The same is true with social contacts or when one meets a man or woman on the street. We go through courteous formalities, "Good morning, Sir. How are you? Fine. Nice to see you. Have a great day." But these may not reflect what we truly feel or what we are really suffering.

Yet, in the private place of the pastor's study, people yearn for opportunity to take down the barriers, to unwind, to remove the masks. They want to lay their souls bare and to find relief from the terrible pressures of life. Yes, here in the private place, God's men meet people under all kinds of circumstances indeed.

A mother worrying over a wayward son, a wife who suspects her husband of unfaithfulness, a teenager who thinks she is pregnant, a child who feels inferior, a father contemplating suicide because he cannot find work, a young man who confesses to having stolen from his employer, a girl who hates her father and who finally confesses to his sexual abuse, a saint of the church who has become hooked on prescription drugs, a man who is involved in narcotics—all these and more are circumstances under which the pastor confronts people in the private place. These circumstances lend value to the meeting. They make it all the more important that the minister do his task well and that the minister be in touch with God. There may not be another opportunity. What will happen in the future will depend very much on how the first session is conducted, the rapport established, the boundaries set, the battle plan laid out.

Truth of the matter is, the man of God is offering a rare commodity. He offers hope to those who have lost hope. He offers help to those who feel past being helped. He is in many cases the last resort, though he ought not be, and he brings to bear on the situation not human resources but all the resources of God. That is why the private place is so important, why it must be taken seriously, why no minister can afford to go into the private place casually or half-heartedly.

It is a serious and awesome responsibility for the minister to be positioned where he points the way to God, to forgiveness, to deliverance, to a brighter day. But such is the work of God's minister when he counsels men and women on matters of the human heart. Such is the awesome responsibility and such also the tremendous joy and satisfaction when daybreak comes after the darkness.

REWARDS OF THE PRIVATE LIFE

Equal to the importance of the private place are the rewards which come to the minister who does the job well. When the minister sees people survive crisis, when he witnesses the spiritual victory which is theirs through Jesus Christ, when he walks with them through the valley and sees them emerge victoriously on the other side, then he also shares in the joy. He too shares in the rewards.

The minister who gives himself fully to counseling, to a ministry of love and concern for individuals as opposed to the public display of that love, will reap unexpected rewards in terms of the human heart.

It was Sunday morning of pastor appreciation day. The minister stood at the door of his church, bidding his parishioners goodbye and shaking hands. Many people came through the door on this particular Sunday—young and old, all smiling, wishing him well. But one of them struck a special note in his heart. There was Jerry, now twenty years old and married. Jerry who but a few years ago ran away from home. Jerry whom the pastor had once gotten out of jail, whom he had worked with for months in the solitude of the private place, whom he had seen grow out of the wildness and the loneliness of adolescence. Jerry whom he had one day married to a lovely girl. That girl now stood with Jerry and little Debbie was toddling. Jerry was now dressed nicely, eyes sparkling. He had a fine job. Was well on his way to a successful and productive life. Most of all he had found peace with God.

The pastor received a special nudge of the Holy Spirit when he shook Jerry's hand. There were others. Most were products of the private place. They said, "I love you, Pastor," in a special way on this morning. And the pastor knew what a great reward it really was.

Besides the reward of inner satisfaction, the joy of sharing on a personal basis, the pastor who ministers in the private place is rewarded by seeing his influence grow and his reputation spread far beyond normal realms. There is no advertisement like that of someone telling a friend, "We have a pastor who can be trusted. He really came through for me. If you ever need a friend, I can recommend him without question."

A successful pastor seldom knows where the phone calls originate, where the people are found. They come from the fertile soil of his counseling, friend to friend, built upon the fruits of his labors over many years. It is a reward the young envy, a reward the blind and the insensitive never understand.

Then too we must not forget the eternal rewards which come to those who faithfully carry out the Master's commission on this earth. Jesus reminded us that not one cup of water would be given in His name without being rewarded. Counseling is a ministry of water to the thirsty. It is a stooping to those who desperately need a friend. It is a binding up of wounds and a caring for the depressed in a most unusual way. The true man of God simply cannot take this ministry lightly.

Even if the rewards here seem negligible, even if the crowds are not at one's door, and the people seem rather cool to all the hard work, even if the denomination seems to ignore that you are struggling in your little corner of the world, the minister must keep in mind that God sees. God knows every prayer, every agonizing decision, every suffering moment when the minister feels the pain of others. And God will reward. He is just and cannot fail to keep promise with His children. That eternal reward is not to be forgotten.

On the great day of judgment, when all men stand before the Lord, far better it will be to stand with souls who verify faithfulness to ministry than to stand with earthly success or with materialistic accomplishments. If there is one single thing which ministers in today's world need to remember, it would seem to be the spiritual nature of the task which is before us. Here, in this area, only God keeps the records and only God will give the rewards. For some men on this earth, that is enough.

5

THE ALTAR

James A. Cross

INTRODUCTION

Our Christian concept of altar differs significantly from the understanding held by Jews of Old Testament days. To them, the altar spoke of the sacrifices of animals and of burnt offerings which were an atonement for their sins and transgressions (Hebrew Kapher, a covering Exodus 30:10).

The blood of animal sacrifices could never make the petitioner perfect. Only Jesus Christ, who offered himself as a perfect sacrifice could bear man's sins away. On Calvary He suffered, bled, died and rose again to cleanse us from our sins and to set us free.

Thus, we Christians have an altar far better than the Old Testament altars and the earthly tabernacle (Hebrews 13:10-13). Our true Christian altar is a place in the heavenlies, a place of sacrifice where God was propitiated, and where man was forgiven and cleansed of sin. Our real altar is a meeting place between God and man, whereby we enjoy forgiveness and fellowship with our heavenly Father and with our savior Jesus Christ. Our altar is a place where the issues of life and death are settled. Three parties may thus be involved at the heavenly altar: God, who hears and graciously answers; the penitent, who seeks forgiveness and blessing; and interested Christians, who come boldly in Jesus' name, requesting mercy for themselves or for others.

The altar which we have today is symbolic of that true,

heavenly altar, not a place of blood sacrifice but of live petitions. It is probable that the modern custom of having altars in our church buildings originated among the Methodists. The great revivals resulting from camp meetings during 1800-1801 made use of altars. The early Methodists also referred to the altar as the "mourners' bench."

Charles C. Sellers in his book *Lorenzo Dow: The Bearer of the Word*, relates the following about altars in camp meetings. "There was a camp meeting ground on almost every circuit—a grove with a preaching stand and logs arranged before it for seats; around the stand (pulpit) there was a rail, forming the 'altar' where anxious-minded mourners and seekers came."

In the meeting where Peter Cartwright was saved it was reported that, "The power of God was wonderfully displayed; scores of sinners fell under the preaching like men slain in battle; Christians shouted for joy."

THE MINISTER'S ALTAR IS WHERE HE FIRST MEETS GOD.

The Pentecostal idea of an altar is a place where one meets God in response to conviction of sin through the work of the Holy Ghost. Paul's altar was on the road to Damascus (Acts 9:1-6). The Ethiopian eunuch's altar was in his chariot as he was returning home from Jerusalem (Acts 8:27-37). The Philippian jailor's altar was the jail itself and his home (Acts 16:25-34). John Bunyan's altar was at his home while reading the Bible (Romans 3:24) and he wrote of his conversion, "the troubled soul found that he was come unto Mount Zion and unto the city of the Living God."

Peter Cartwright, who later became a famous Methodist minister, found his altar during an outdoor camp meeting in Kentucky. As a sixteen-year-old youth he had already become a wicked sinner—gambling, drinking, and racing horses. He relates his experience as follows: "I went with the weeping multitudes and bowed before the stand and earnestly prayed for mercy. In the midst of a solemn struggle of soul, an impression was made on my mind as though a voice said to me, 'Thy sins are forgiven thee.' Divine light flashed all around me. Unspeakable joy sprang up in my soul. I have never for one moment, doubted that the Lord did then and there forgive my sins."

My own altar of repentance and salvation was by the side of a bed with my father on one side and my mother on the other. As a teenager, late one night after returning from revival services, conviction seized my heart. That night, in the month of May, 1924, is forever etched in my memory. As I confessed to God, and as tears of repentance coursed down my cheeks, God for Christ's sake heard my prayers and made me a new creature. Condemnation and guilt lifted from my soul and a new name was written down in glory.

THE ALTAR IS A PLACE WHICH MUST NOT BE FORGOTTEN.

That place where we first met God must never be forgotten. Its memories are too precious, and the great transaction which took place there is too momentous for us ever to let it fade as the great experience of our life. Its recall should always remain part of our testimony of thanksgiving. David cried aloud, "He brought me up also out of an horrible pit, out of the miry clay, and set my feet upon a rock, and established my goings. And he hath put a new song in my mouth, even praise unto our God . . ." (Psalm 40:2, 3).

Paul recalled his conversion experience, his altar, before the multitude after he was seized by the Jews in the temple. In detail he told of the great light that shone from heaven, and of the voice of the Lord who spoke to him. Even though twenty-six years had rolled over his head since that wonderful day, it seemed as fresh as the day it happened. Two years later, two years of bonds and imprisonment, Paul stood before King Agrippa and in words of testimony he again revisited the place and circumstances of his conversion. Time, bonds, imprisonments—not anything could dim Paul's vision of Christ's sacrifice, nor diminish the joy of his salvation. Paul never forgot the place of his altar and he often returned to that hallowed place in his prayers and during his preaching.

Having known a personal altar of repentance and transformation, Paul could preach to others form an experiential standpoint. He declared to the Corinthians, "Christ died for our sins according to the Scriptures" (1 Corinthians 15:3). He also stated, "I am determined not to know anything among you save Jesus Christ, and Him crucified" (1 Corinthians 2:2).

Paul could clearly point them to the way of salvation from the Holy Scriptures and also from a personal, tried, and satisfactory relationship with God in his own life. As a minister, one of our rewarding joys is telling people of an altar of reconciliation, and then seeing those to whom we have preached find their way into that spiritual holy of holies, the very presence of a forgiving God.

THE ALTAR IS A PLACE OF PERSONAL DEVOTION.

To be a herald of the good news, the minister must know intimately what comprises the good news. To attempt to preach when one does not know the gospel may be compared to Ahimaaz who wished to run with Cushi, "And Joab said, wherefore wilt thou run my son, seeing that thou hast no tidings ready?" (2 Samuel 18:22).

Thus, every minister is required to spend much time in the study of God's Word. Jesus commissioned His followers: "Go ye therefore into all the world and preach the gospel to every creature" (Mark 16:15). The Good News *must* be preached. Paul wrote, "It pleased God by the foolishness of preaching to save them that believe" (1 Corinthians 1:21).

Every minister must be a man of the Word. The Bible is the book he must spend time and effort in learning, because this is the book he attempts to explain. No minister of the Word of God can be excused for not having knowledge and understanding of the Word. A. W. Tozer in his book, *Man, The Dwelling Place of God,* writes "Every Christian should master the Bible, or at least spend hours and days and years trying." Dr. Jowett writes in his book, *The Preacher; His Life and Work,* "I would urge upon all young preachers amid all their reading, to be always engaged in the comprehensive study of some one book of the Bible."

It is at this point where that altar of personal devotion becomes so meaningful to the minister.

The art of meditation on God's Word is largely lost in today's world. We rush through days of split-second timing, instant news, instant food, and all too often instant sermon material provided from multi-sources. But the psalmist said of the good man, "But his delight is in the law of the Lord; and in his law doth he meditate day and night" (Psalm 1:2). He went on to say, "O how I love thy law, it is my meditation all the day" (Psalm 119:97). "I will meditate in thy precepts" (Psalm 119:15).

Today's minister must take time at the altar to read God's Word, to think about what he has read, to ponder over it, to let the Holy Spirit minister as he meditates, and to let the Spirit enlighten his soul.

While at the altar of personal devotions, it is good to meditate carefully upon Paul's words, "Preach the WORD" (1 Timothy 4:2). This charge given by the Apostle Paul probably represents some of his last words, preserved especially for these days. The charge is, "Preach the Word"; not our theories, our opinions or our philosophies. The thing that will count in that day of all days is the WORD. Therefore, for ministers of the gospel, the altar must be a place given to much reading and study of God's Word.

The altar of personal devotion may include times of quiet thought and waiting on God: "But when thou prayest, enter into thy closet, and when thou hast shut the door, pray to thy Father which is in secret; and thy Father which seeth in secret shall reward thee openly" (Matthew 6:6). The psalmist wrote, "Be still and know that I am God" (Psalm 46:10). He is the king of all hosts. He is with us. He is our refuge. How very necessary it is for us to be still and recognize this tremendous truth. Such awareness affords consolation in a world of grief, hope in despair, refuge in times of deep trouble. We must take time to wait on God. We need to cease from our fretful labor, and to just step back and watch God perform His wonderful work.

There are moments when words are not necessary to convey meaning, feeling, and love. My wife and I have been married for over fifty years. We know and understand one another. Our tastes and our thoughts are similar in so many ways. Sometimes we like to just sit with each other. Reading material is put away, the news cast is turned off, and distracting sounds are shut out. Quietness envelopes us in these moments. It is not necessary to tell each other our feelings. A gentle squeeze of the hand or a gesture conveys the current of deep love we have for one another.

How much more does the minister need to spend time alone with Jesus, adoring Him, and experiencing His loving nearness. Such moments bring unspeakable joy and they add stability and spiritual maturity which others will notice.

The altar of personal devotions may require times of agonizing intercessory prayer. Paul exhorts that, "First of all, supplications, prayers, intercession, and giving of thanks be made for all men" (1 Timothy 2:1). Intercession means prayer on behalf of another. Prayer to God on behalf of others may grow into a regular service ministry of a preacher of the Word.

While at his altar, a true minister of God may sometimes be impelled to allow the Holy Spirit to intercede on behalf of someone's special need or on behalf of the church. In both the Old Testament and the New Testament the Bible abounds with examples of intercessory prayer. I submit only a few.

After Israel had sinned in worshiping the golden calf made by Aaron, Moses interceded with God to spare His people (Exodus 32:11-14). Moses also interceded on behalf of Miriam that she be healed of her leprosy (Exodus 12:13).

At the dedication of the Temple, King Solomon prayed on behalf of the people of Israel (1 Kings 8:22-53). Jesus prayed a powerful intercessory prayer for believers (John 17:9, 11, 15, 17-21). As He hung on the cross he interceded on behalf of those who crucified him (Luke 23:34).

Paul interceded for the nation of Israel, that it would be saved (Romans 10:1).

The Church interceded in behalf of Peter who was in prison (Acts 12:5).

The Holy Spirit intercedes through believers at times when we cannot express our thoughts and do not know how to pray or for what to pray (Romans 8:26-27).

What unbounded joy one finds at the altar of personal devotions when we hear of answers to such prayers. In his book, *Prayer Power Unlimited.* J. Oswald Sanders wrote, "In intercession there are reflex benefits to the one who prays as well as direct benefits to the one for whom intercession is made."

The altar of personal devotion may entail weeping, fasting, and deep soul searching. Paul tells the Ephesian Church, "I have been with you at all seasons, serving the Lord with all humility of mind, and with many tears" (Acts 20:18b-19a). It is a joy to be able to weep before the Lord and to "weep with them that weep" (Romans 12:15).

The altar of devotion may be bathed with tears for lost loved ones. We may weep over heartbreaks, on behalf of one who is ill, or for those burdened or tempted. But what joy to know God sees our tears. David requested the Lord to, "put thou my tears into thy bottle: are they not in thy book?" (Psalm 56:8). The song poet admonishes us to "weep o'er the erring ones, lift up the fallen." The Psalmist David promises that, "They that sow in tears shall reap in joy. He that goeth forth and weepeth, bearing precious seed, shall doubtless come again with rejoicing, bringing his sheaves with him" (Psalm 126:5-6). And God our Father has promised that the day will come when He will wipe away all tears and we shall sorrow no more (Revelation 7:17; 21:4).

The altar of personal devotion may call for periods of fasting. In terms of the New Testament the question is not whether we should fast. Fasting is expected. Jesus said, "But thou when thou fastest, anoint thy head and wash thy face" (Matthew 6:17). Fasting seems to have been a way of life, a part of devotion, in early church life. Prayer is almost always linked with fasting (Acts 17:23). Paul admonishes, "give yourselves to fasting and prayer" (1 Corinthians 7:5). Paul also laid down some conduct qualifications for preachers where he speaks of approving ourselves in fasting (2 Corinthians 6:5). Jesus tells us that certain evil spirits cannot be cast out except by prayer and fasting (Matthew 17:21; Mark 9:29).

Of course, fasting is never to be an ostentatious observance (Matthew 6:16). It is not an endurance contest of which to boast. However preachers of the gospel are expected to follow the example our Chief Shepherd gave us, and joyously spend time in fasting and praying. The joy of seeing precious results is more than worth the conflict between the flesh and spirit.

In the heart of every God-called minister there is perennial thirsting for God and the things of the Spirit. David expresses it this way, "As the deer pants for the water brooks, so pants my soul for you, O God. My soul thirsts for God, for the living God" (Psalm 42:1-2, *New King James Version*).

Jesus said this passage from John's gospel, "In the last day, that great day of the feast Jesus stood and cried saying, If any man thirst let him come unto me and drink. He that believeth on me as the Scripture hath said, out of his belly shall flow rivers of living water" (John 7:37-38).

Jesus challenges every thirst in every man, and He promises that the thirst will be satisfied. At the personal altar of devotion we can drink again and again of God's boundless Spirit.

No doubt there was a multitude of people who heard this invitation of our Lord. It was on an individual basis, "any man"; but it also separated and qualified. The individual must be thirsty. He must believe on Jesus as the scriptures have said. G. Campbell points out some beautiful thoughts concerning verse eight. "How many people are in that verse? You never know. Supposing I hear that call and obey it; my thirst quenched, then what? Out of me the rivers flow, and how far they will flow I shall never know, how many people's thirst will be quenched from the river flowing out of my life, because I am satisfied with Jesus, no one will ever know. We become channels through whom the overflowing rivers should pass. As long as I am a thirsty soul, I can supply no rivers that quench the thirst of other souls."

So let us go to our altars, O men of God. Let us stay until showers from on high fill every thirsting pore, and until we soak in refreshing blessings of God, blessings which banish heartaches and lift burdens. Let us stay at our altars until joy flows like a river and until we can sing:

> "Like the rain that falls from heaven,
> Like the sunlight from the sky,
> So, the Holy Ghost is given,
> Coming on us from on high.
>
> See a fruitful field is growing,
> Blessed fruits of righteousness,
> And the streams of life are flowing,
> In a lonely wilderness."

The altar is a place of confrontation with God and self. Every preacher of the gospel needs a private place, an altar, where he can face God alone. It may be the study where the door can be locked and everything and everybody excluded. It may be on some mountain top, or in a car while traveling, or on a boat, or in the woods; but it must be a place where you make God welcome into your heart.

Jacob visited this altar beside the brook Jabbok (Genesis 32).

Returning home after an absence of twenty years, his journey was interrupted. His own messengers brought disturbing news that his brother Esau was coming to meet him with four hundred men. Memories were vividly recalled. Esau's threat to kill him, made twenty years earlier, would now come to pass. Jacob prayed for deliverance for his family, household goods, servants, personal wealth, and himself. He formulated a strategy which he hoped would appease Esau's wrath and effect a reconciliation.

That night Jacob sent everyone and everything he owned over the ford Jabbok. He remained alone. Jacob knew that all his scheming plans, bold posturings, or outward pretense would be of no help to him that night. He faced God and he finally confessed to God what he had been, and what he was—a trickster, a deceiver, a sinner. What a night! Following his confession, his nakedness of soul before God, Jacob became a changed man.

Isaiah found this altar in the temple where, before the holiness of God, he confessed his shortcomings and experienced a touch of fire that transformed his life (Isaiah 6).

While the minister is not *of* the world, he lives *in* the world with all of its sin. He faces not only his own problems, but those of his members. He must give them counsel, listen to their problems, bear them up in prayer, and keep their secrets buried in his bosom. Sometimes the minister is misunderstood, even by his fellow clergymen. He faces a cold, hostile world, battles unclean spirits until he is almost drained spiritually, and may feel as Elijah when fleeing from Jezebel. During such times as these the preacher needs to get alone with God, face to face, and to bare himself before his Maker. He must not cover up or withhold from God; but pray as did David, "O Lord, thou hast searched me, and known me. Thou knowest my downsitting and mine uprising, thou understandest my thoughts afar off. Thou compassest my path and my lying down, and art acquainted with all my ways. For there is not a word in my tongue, but, lo, O Lord, thou knowest altogether" (Psalm 139:1-4).

While face to face, shut in with God, the minister will find it beneficial to lay it all out. We must let Christ bear our burdens. Tell Him about our disappointments. Confess to Him our failures, and examine our strengths and weaknesses in

His presence. If the church is not making the progress it should, let us inquire of God as to the reason. Let's be honest with God and be willing to come to grips with the problem. Let's ask God about the resolution and how to solve the problem.

Have we been faithful in our efforts to reach God's throne and in our search for His power to work through us? Have we been spending enough time in the presence of God to let Him saturate us with His glory? We find surprising and sometimes miraculous answers at this altar of confrontation. Here lies the path to power, a route that will affect our church and the entire community. At this altar eternal things become very personal. This fleeting life and fading world become less important when we kneel before God the Eternal One.

It is the minister's duty to deal with spiritual matters. He deals with souls destined to inhabit eternity, and the preacher must realize that in his hands rests the futures of people who will spend eternity in either heaven or hell. At his altar the minister realizes keenly that he shall be required to answer to God about his work for the Kingdom. He shall give an account of his stewardship.

This materialistic world would press our ministry into its mold and cause us to think like worldlings. Great danger lies in comparing our successes with business successes of the world.

But at this altar of facing God we choose God's priorities as our own. God's values become our values. We stop comparing ourselves with ourselves, and we focus on Jesus the perfect one. And when we look Him full in the face, "The things of earth become strangely dim, in the light of His glory and grace."

There are some real joys which result from this confrontation with God and self. It may be that we find the source of personal power and victory. This could be the place where we receive power to go out and accomplish things we never thought possible. This could be the place where we learn how to come to the pulpit with fire burning on our heart's altar, thus causing us to preach with heavenly power. Here we may learn how to lead God's church through very difficult problems.

If we tarry long enough at this altar, we can come forth with victory and ability for the hour.

Any preacher who goes often to face God will go out from God's presence to find victories in his own personal life. While there is no glamour or praise of men to be heard at our altar of confrontation, it yet takes such a secret confrontation with God to gain success.

We preachers are ambassadors for Christ. We have a commission to preach the gospel to all people so that they may hear and believe on the Lord. We are not perfect. But God loves us in spite of our imperfections, our blunders, and our failures. One day Jesus will present us to the Father without spot or wrinkle and we will hear Him say, "Well done, thou good and faithful servant."

The altar is where the shepherd intercedes for His flock. The true shepherd intercedes often in behalf of those people committed to his care. Moses often prayed for Israel. He wanted God to spare them judgment. He asked that God not destroy them but that He continue His care over them (Exodus 32:9-14). When the people wanted meat in the wilderness, Moses prayed and God answered (Numbers 11:31, 32). When God sent fiery serpents among them, Moses prayed and God gave instructions for their healing (Numbers 21:4-9).

The Lord's disciples, preparing to win souls, were found at an altar in the upper room. It is recorded: "These all continued with one accord in prayer and supplication" (Acts 1:14). From that altar they went out to turn the world upside down for Christ.

When administrative duties interfered with soul-winning, the apostles chose seven men to take care of serving the tables. They declared: "But we will give ourselves continually to prayer and to the ministry of the Word" (Acts 6:4). No church activity, regardless of merit, must be allowed to replace time spent in prayer before God on behalf of the flock.

Dick Eastman said, "The person who weeps in prayer before standing in the pulpit is indeed wise" (Taken from *No Easy Road*). On one occasion, several Salvation Army officers asked General Booth, "How can we win the lost?" Booth's answer, "Try tears."

William Bramwells, a Methodist minister, was known widely

for his personal holiness and success in preaching. His success was a result of his prayer life. It was said of him that he would pray for hours at a time. He went forth on his circuits like a flame of fire. Thousands were converted to Christ in his meetings and many sick were healed in answer to his prayers.

One of the contributing factors in the success of Finney's revivals was a man by the name of Daniel Nash. Nash was a man of much prayer and travail. He would precede Finney to the place of an announced revival, get a room, lock the door, and pray. Instead of his going out, meals would be placed at his door. Sometimes he would stop long enough to eat, but many times the meal would not be touched. For hours, day and night, he prayed to God in behalf of the lost. When Finney arrived and the meeting began, Nash continued his praying. His labor in prayer would continue until revival came. Then he would leave, going to the next city or town and praying on behalf of revival.

Not many people knew Daniel Nash—he was not popular as was Finney—but God knew him. He was not a platform personality but he was a prayer warrior who lay before God in behalf of lost souls. It is said that his clothes were shabby and worn, but his prayers aided many souls in shedding their rags for robes of righteousness. What was his reward? A share in those thousands of souls Charles Finney won to God.

Paul writes Timothy, "I will therefore that men pray everywhere . . ." (1 Timothy 2:8). He opened this chapter with, "I exhort therefore that first of all, supplications, intercessions, and giving of thanks be made for all men" (1 Timothy 2:1). The shepherd is urged to pray for *all* men—saved, unsaved, lost, the backslider, at all times and in every place. We are to tell the good news, and pray that men will accept the gospel.

Oswald J. Smith in his book, *The Revival We Need*, wrote, "Conversion is the operation of the Holy Spirit, and prayer is the power that secures that operation. Souls are not saved by man but by God, and since He works in answer to prayer we have no choice but to follow the Divine plan. Prayer moves the arm that moves the world." The altar of prayer and intercession must never be forsaken.

The prophet Joel proclaimed a message for today's true shepherds: "Let the priest, the ministers of the Lord weep between the porch and altar, and let them say, spare thy people O Lord . . ." (Joel 2:17). So again I say, let us go to the altar of intercession, O men of God, "Blow the trumpet in Zion, sanctify a fast, call a solemn assembly" (Joel 2:15).

Today's shepherd must be as concerned over his people, whom the Lord has committed to his care, as was Moses for Israel, and as was Paul for his kindred (Romans 9:3). These days call for men of compassion, for men concerned about souls who will live in eternity. We need men of intercession who will call for God to save his people from these evil days, and send revival to our churches. It is not new plans, or new methods, or new programs which we need. Such are helpful but not vital. Of paramount importance is the need for shepherds whom God can use, for men who are strong and mighty in prayer. The Holy Ghost flows through men who will give themselves completely to God, men who will be golden pipes through which oil can flow unhindered.

E. M. Bounds, in *Power Through Prayer,* writes of present day shepherds: "We shut ourselves to our study, we become bookworms, Bible worms, sermon makers, noted for literature, thought and sermons; but the people and God, where are they? Out of heart, out of mind. Preachers who are great thinkers, great students, must be the greatest men of prayer or else they will be less than the least of preachers in God's estimate."

Let the shepherd intercede and weep before God. Let him follow the example of Joel, Moses, Jesus and Paul. Such intercession must be fervent and in faith: "Elias was a man (underline man) subject to like passions as we are, and he *prayed earnestly* that it might not rain, and it rained not on the earth by the space of three years and six months. And he prayed again and the heaven gave rain, and the rain brought forth her fruit" (James 5:17-18).

Our intercession must be definite and to the point. We must pray for "my sheep," and we must petition, "spare thy people." The prayer of faith is a definite request, made in definite faith, for a definite answer. Persist in your intercession. Do not give up because you do not see an immediate answer. Elijah prayed seven times before his servant saw and reported a cloud about the size of a man's hand. But rain finally came.

Always remember, "Weeping may endure for a night, but *JOY* cometh in the morning" (Psalm 30:5). "They that sow in tears shall reap in *JOY*" (Psalm 126:5). Time spent at the altar of intercession is repaid in joy. The shepherd who earnestly prays for revival experiences great joy when souls are born into the kingdom of God. To the minister who tarries long before the Lord, it is a joy when a refreshed people rejoice. Such a shepherd also knows there are some snatched as it were from the burning, and he shouts aloud, "It's worth it all."

THE ALTAR IS WHERE VICTORY IS WON.

The altar is where the victory is won. One of the most graphic and dramatic examples of the altar where victory is won we find in the first book of Kings. It was a battle between God and Satan, between Jehovah and Baal, between many prophets of an idol god Baal and one lone prophet of the living Lord. A very decisive victory was won at that altar (1 Kings 18:30-39).

There are significant things worth mentioning about Elijah's altar on Mount Carmel.

Elijah repaired the altar of the Lord. Many think that an altar had occupied this spot in past days. Some believe Abraham or Samuel may have had an altar here. Some believe that, during the time of the judges, an altar had occupied Carmel. Whatever, the altar was repaired.

Twelve stones were used to represent the twelve tribes of Israel, indicating that all Israel was united in the worship of God. Wood was laid on the altar and the offering was slain and placed on the wood. Twelve barrelsful of water were poured over the sacrifice. Wood and sacrifice were drenched and water ran into a trench around the altar. For fire to consume the sacrifice under such circumstances appeared to be an impossibility. But Elijah prayed and the fire fell. Victory was achieved in an exceptional manner.

Clarke's Commentary points out: 1. Fire came down from heaven. No possibility of concealed fire. 2. The pieces of the ssacrifice were consumed first. 3. The wood burned next, to show that it was not even by means of the wood that the flesh was burned. 4. The twelve stones were also consumed to show it was no common fire, but one whose agency nothing could resist. 5. The dust of the earth was burned up. 6. The water that was in the trench was burned up.

Such total victory was acknowledged even by the enemies of the Lord who declared, "The Lord, He is God."

It does not matter how difficult the problem, or how sore the battle, there is victory in the altar. When Joshua faced five kings and their armies, he prayed and it is written, "And there was no day like that before it, or after it, that the Lord hearkened unto the voice of a man: for the Lord fought for Israel" (Joshua 10:14). When Moab and Ammon came to battle against Jehoshaphat, the Bible records, "And Jehoshaphat . . . set himself to seek the Lord, and proclaimed a fast throughout all Judah and Judah gathered themselves together, to ask help of the Lord: even out of all the cities of Judah they came to seek the Lord" (2 Chronicles 20:2-3). They came to the altar where victory is won and it worked: "The Lord fought against the enemies of Israel" (2 Chronicles 20:29).

Let us rejoice, O men of God, that we have an altar that is mighty through God. God loves us and desires to give us victory over all our foes. We must never forsake the altar because this is where victory is won.

One memorable experience at the altar occurred for me when a lady member of my church was ill with cancer. The doctor gave her three months to live. One Sunday night the lady's husband brought her to church. During prayer for the sick, Charles carried his wife to the altar in his arms. She was too weak to walk. I called for the saints to come for prayer. We anointed her with oil. As many as could laid hands on her and God's healing power was present.

More than thirty years later I was preaching a revival in Florida where this same lady was present. During the service she rose to testify and related the incident of her healing WITH GREAT JOY.

Yes, the altar is where the victory is won.

One of the greatest joys of my ministry has been seeing people saved from sin and walking with the Lord. I have experienced the joy of knowing many who lived the Christian life successfully and made it home to glory.

Paul expressed it in this manner. "For what is our hope, or joy, or crown of rejoicing? Are not even ye in the presence of the Lord Jesus at His coming? For ye are our glory and joy" (1 Thessalonians 2:19-20).

The toil and labor of the altar returns abundant joy. I have met people who were saved in revivals I conducted more than fifty years ago, people who are yet living for God, and who are continuing in their faithful service for Jesus. I have met ministers who were converted under my preaching and who are and have been winning others to God. The benefits of the altar are thus multiplied and I can join Paul in saying, "These are my glory and joy."

CONCLUSION

In closing let us note there are altars for times of crisis, such as Jacob found. There are also altars of reconsecration, such as when Jacob later returned to Bethel. And there are neglected, fallen altars which need to be re-built in order for the fire of the Lord to fall.

Paul could accept his thorn in the flesh after earnest, prolonged prayer at the altar. He had assurance from God, "My grace is sufficient for thee: for my strength is made perfect in weakness." Paul's attitude towards his affliction was corrected as a result, and he could say, "most gladly therefore will I rather glory in my infirmities that the power of Christ may rest upon me" (2 Corinthians 12:9). Paul was able to accept all circumstances of life connected with his ministry, both favorable and unfavorable (Philippians 4:11-13). He was assured of his ability, through Christ, to accomplish all things for God's glory (Philippians 4:13).

So are we assured of victoriously overcoming (Romans 8:37). We are confident that we can live victoriously in this present world, and that the same power which saved us will keep us until Jesus comes or calls (Philippians 1:6).

THANK GOD FOR THE ALTAR!

6

TIMES OF CRISES

Harold E. Stevens

INTRODUCTION

The minister must not look at circumstances in themselves, but to his relationship with Jesus Christ. This was the apostle Paul's attitude. He did not look at Christ through his circumstances. He looked at circumstances through Christ. Joy in ministry comes when we have our circumstances working for us rather than against us. When we do this, joy can be ours always.

TIMES OF CRISIS

Even during times of crisis, a minister can have joy in his ministry. It is at this moment when the minister draws on all his resources. The crisis may often become his finest hour. Self-confidence, faith, optimism—these may all be faked when life is going well; but, in a crisis, the minister is challenged to his limit. The challenge often proves the real presence or absence of these spiritual qualities demanded of the successful minister.

When it comes to his pastoral work, a Christian pastor may seek to help in crisis, or he may consciously or unconsciously attempt to avoid it. Whichever, it is something which cannot be avoided for long. Pastors simply must be with their people during the rough moments of life. Therefore, the pastor will either effectively carry out this part of his work or he will do a poor job. This is the proving ground. There are many things a minister can avoid by controlling his schedule and budgeting his time, but crises ministry is not one of them. Crises must be handled when they happen. Herein may lie the secret to ministerial success. It may be the crossroads determining whether the minister will have deep spiritual joy while ministering in the moment of crisis or whether he will know such pain and frustration that it may eventually take him out of ministry. A minister cannot prepare for every event he will face in life, but he must make an effort to properly equip himself for dealing with crisis.

I have often known ministers who appeared to handle their ministries well. Then suddenly a crisis developed and they immediately gave up and resigned. Self-concept did not allow these men to remain and work through the crisis. If they could have worked through the crisis, they would have learned a great deal about life.

Unfortunately a minister may resign in times of pastoral conflict rather than hanging on and realizing the positive aspects of the battle. The conflict may be very difficult to deal with; but staying with the situation, rather than running from it, will give the minister new insight about himself and about people and the dynamics that cause them to respond in certain ways. Also, it is during conflict that the minister will draw closer to God, whereas resigning—not dealing with the crisis—can have a negative affect on all future relationships in that he misses the positive things he could have experienced.

The novice minister may think only other people become involved in crisis. He may suddenly find himself facing a personal crisis of his own.

It is not uncommon for a minister to face a crisis of faith. Did not Jeremiah face such a crisis? He wrote, "I am in derision daily, every one mocketh me . . . then I said, I will not make mention of him, nor speak any more in his name" (Jeremiah 20:7, 9). Moses, Elijah, Peter—many other Bible characters also had a personal crisis of faith. Yet they survived. That is the important matter.

A minister's personal crisis may come in different ways. It may involve his marriage, his children, his finances, or his health. Either of these are often intensified by the minister's responsibility as a public servant.

At present there is a host of misguided if not false teachers espousing a wrong emphasis on positive thinking, divine health, name it and claim it, and hyped-up success stories beyond number. Let us note also that the crisis is often made worse by guilt complexes which come from what these teachers are saying. Regardless of all these teachings, and all efforts to play down these moments of crisis, they do not go away easily: the minister must learn to face up to them.

The minister knows what he is dealing with is very real. Resolutions of the problems cannot be faked. A minister need not be considered a fatalist or a negative person just because he recognizes that crises will come. We find proof of this in the examples of Job, Stephen, and Paul. Does not even tradition remind us that all the apostles, except John, died by being put to death for their faith? The minister will face personal crises. In all of this, however, he is not to cave in. He learns to stand firm, to cope, to survive, and even to experience joy.

Not only does the minister face crises of his own, but he is also forced to confront crises in the lives of others.

Homes fracture due to social pressure. Communication between family members breaks down. Spiritual deficiencies arise, plus numerous other problems. The minister is usually the "helping" person called on to assist in coping with these pressures. Also, in some homes there will be sickness, ranging from mild depression to acute mental disorders, not to mention those crises which stem from accidents, and from the stress of dealing with aging parents, death, and bereavement. All these fall in on the minister in today's world, sometimes with overwhelming force, and he must have strength beyond himself if he hopes to survive and bless others.

It may not seem easy for the minister to find joy even during times of bereavement. Death involves separation, grief, loneliness, loss, and a number of other emotions; yet it may at the same time furnish us a beautiful example of how the Holy Spirit comforts both the dying and the minister.

Doris (not her real name, though the situation is factual) was a woman in her early fifties when she became a victim of cancer. She entered the hospital, underwent surgery, and later returned home. Approximately one year passed. The cancer reoccurred. Doris was hospitalized again. More surgery. Another stay at home. Then a final return to the hospital. Death was near. Doris asked many searching questions, prayed fervent prayers, and made diligent efforts to have someone pray the prayer of faith in her behalf. Nevertheless, she went on to be with the Lord.

During Doris' long struggle I visited her often and allowed her to talk. At first, she talked of health, not of dying. I never in any way discouraged this, nor did I try to change her thoughts. Early one morning she called for me. My wife and I went to the hospital.

She said, "It looks like it's about over," as we entered the room.

"And what does that mean to you?" I asked.

She smiled and said, "I'm not afraid."

With that statement and others like it, the Comforter brought peace and joy to Doris. The same peace filled the hearts of those of us who were present in the room. As she moved from the subject of healing to the promises of God for the dying, the Holy Spirit sealed the Word to her heart. A worshipful attitude prevailed. As Doris triumphed and entered into the presence of the Lord, we all experienced joy. Joy came to me especially as the minister, for God allowed me to be a facilitator for His wonderful plan.

There are other times when the joy of ministering comes through watching and leading others to higher ground and personal victory. Many people are controlled by their past. They seem to have little or no power over the negative things which happened to them when they were younger. Joy will fill any minister's life when he helps a person deal with, and overcome, these negatives. This is often a long process, requiring patience and understanding, but great joy comes when victory is finally won.

With Jane's permission (not her real name) I share the following experience. It helps point out what I mean by leading someone to higher spiritual ground.

Jane, her husband and son moved into our area from another city and began attending the church I pastored. She was very devout, a tremendous worker in the church, but for some reason not a very happy Christian. After being at the church for a good while, and her son beginning to grow up, she and her husband wanted another child. At one point her doctor said she was expecting. It later turned out she was not pregnant but she had to enter the hospital for surgery. The resulting trauma brought on a crisis which prompted her to seek counseling help.

As she entered into counseling, Jane began to gain some insights about her past. Counseling continued over the years, not just a few weeks or months.

Jane's father had died when she was eight years old. She had not been allowed to go to the hospital to see him during his illness. Prior to entering the hospital, he had given Jane a doll and, after his death, this doll became a precious symbol of her father's love. This same doll, however, became a source of contention between Jane and her mother. One day Jane's mother took the doll, placed it in a shoe box, and went to the back of their garage. As Jane watched, she dug a hole and buried the doll, talking to Jane as it was being covered with dirt. "He's gone, Jane. Your father is gone. He won't be back. I want you to forget him. Don't talk about him anymore."

As Jane talked with me, the Holy Spirit allowed her to begin re-living all of this, though she had basically blotted it from her memory.

On the Taylor-Johnson Temperament Analysis Test (a psychological test of personality), she showed a very, very poor self-concept. All those years of unresolved grief had left her with a feeling of inferiority, unhappiness, and a loathing for herself as a human being even though she was a talented, brilliant person.

As Jane counseled with me, the Holy Spirit worked and brought about a tremendous change in her life. She has since earned a college degree. She is at the present time pursuing a Master's Degree in Communications. She is growing more mature in her relationship with God and she continues to be an excellent church worker.

Truly, when you help lead someone to higher ground, there is joy for the minister as well as for the person in pilgrimage.

Even though crises are very difficult, I am made to believe the minister not only should have joy, but he should have it in all circumstances: "Rejoice in the Lord alway: and again I say, Rejoice" (Philippians 4:4).

OUR RELATIONSHIP WITH GOD

True joy is based on a proper relationship with God. It comes as a result of being filled with the Holy Spirit. It is an inward condition that takes place in man's being (spirit), not dependent on external happenings.

Joy may be viewed as distinct from happiness and pleasure. Here is what I mean. Happiness often comes more from our relationships with others. If our relationships are good, we feel good toward others and they feel good toward us. Then we are happy. But such happiness is dependent on circumstances. Pleasure is something that appeals to our senses. If what we are doing pleases the senses, then we are experiencing pleasure.

Joy is a result of a relationship with God. It can only be experienced as we receive God and are filled with His Spirit. Joy in the Lord enhances happiness by giving us a proper foundation for relationships with others. Such spiritual joy enhances pleasure by helping us to put all pleasing sense experiences within a controllable framework.

Thus we, as God's children, are strengthened through the joy of the Lord (Nehemiah 8:10).

A PROPER THEOLOGICAL PERSPECTIVE

To fully understand the joy of ministry one simply must establish a theological understanding of the subject. In the Old Testament, joy is frequently referred to as a religious emotion which finds outward expression in leaping, shouting, and singing. Joy is often looked at as an outcome of a relationship with God. "In thy presence is fulness of joy" (Psalm 16:11). God is at once the source of joy: "Restore unto me the joy of thy salvation" (Psalm 51:12) and also the object of joy: "And my soul shall be joyful in the Lord: it shall rejoice in his salvation" (Psalm 35:9). The phrase, "rejoice (be glad) in God," and similar expressions occur frequently in Scripture. (See Psalms 97:12; 149:2; Isaiah 61:10; Zechariah 10:7.)

In the New Testament, the element of joy in religion is very prevalent and is an appropriate response of the believer to the "good tidings of great joy," which constitute the Gospel (Luke 2:10). Joy is exemplified in Jesus' life and character, as well as set forth in His teachings. There are many indications that in spite of grief and tragedy in the life of Jesus, His demeanor was joyous. We find Him "rejoicing in spirit" (Luke 10:21) and His desire was for His joy to be in His followers (John 15:11; 17:13).

This exuberant state of joy, "Rejoice and be exceeding glad," (Matthew 5:12) is in sharp contrast to the "Sad Countenance," (Matthew 6:16) of the Pharisees. The discerning of the true treasure of life brings joy (Matthew 13:44). Jesus confers on His followers the full participation in His own fullness of joy (John 15:11; 16:24; 17:13). And most blessed of all, the joy we have cannot be removed from us by man: "Your joy no man taketh from you" (John 16:22).

In the dark days following the crucifixion, the disciples passed under a cloud. At the resurrection, joy shown forth again (Luke 24:41). After Pentecost, great joy remained a marked characteristic of the early Church (Acts 2:46; 8:39; 13:52; 15:3).

Paul declares that joy is one of the fruits of the spirit (Galatians 5:22). He said the kingdom of God is, "joy in the Holy Ghost" (Romans 14:17). Peter tells us that, in Christ, the Christian "rejoices with joy unspeakable and full of glory" (1 Peter 1:8).

Christian joy is not gaiety that knows no gloom, but it is the result of the triumph of faith over adverse and trying circumstances. These circumstances, instead of binding, actually enhance the believer's joy.

The apostles rejoiced at being counted worthy to suffer for Christ (Acts 9:41). Paul gloried in tribulation (Romans 5:3). James admonishes us to count it all joy when we are tempted (James 1:2). Peter tells us to rejoice at being able to partake of Christ's suffering (1 Peter 4:13). And even our Lord, "for the joy that was set before him, endured the cross, despising the shame" (Hebrews 12:2). We can readily see that, for every Christian, scriptures place great emphasis upon joy. How much more should this be true for the minister charged with responsibility for leading others into mature Christian living.

THE WORD OF GOD

In today's world where change comes at supersonic speeds, the Christian desperately needs a source where he can obtain joy. This source must be permanent, not changing with each passing day.

Where does the believer find this source?

The answer is God's Word. The comfort of God's Word can be present with us in a changing world. The Word is permanent: "For verily I say unto you, Till heaven and earth pass, one jot or one tittle shall in no wise pass from the law, till all be fulfilled" (Matthew 5:18). The Word is powerful: "So shall my word be that goeth forth out of my mouth: it shall not return unto me void, but it shall accomplish that which I please, and it shall prosper in the thing whereto I sent it" (Isaiah 55:11). The Word gives knowledge: "Now all these things happened unto them for ensamples: and they are written for our admonition" (1 Corinthians 10:11). The Word gives hope: "For whatsoever things were written aforetime were written for our learning, that we through patience and comfort of the scriptures might have hope" (Romans 15:4). And the Word gives comfort: "This is my comfort in my affliction: for thy word hath quickened me" (Psalm 119:50).

Among evangelicals there is little or no argument concerning the value of God's Word. But when we consider it as a source of comfort, do we use the source or do we take it very lightly?

For example, let's examine your involvement with the Scripture by asking a few simple questions. A number of scriptures and locations have been given in this chapter. When you came to a scripture quotation, did you actually read it? or did you speedily pass by because it was scripture and you had read it before? Have you looked up any of the scriptures to see if the location was correctly stated? or even to make sure the statement was in the Bible?

How about other things being read? How do you treat Scripture when it is in a book, an article, or a tract? Do you read it or hurriedly skim over it?

The reason for this probe is to help us evaluate our attitude toward the Word of God. If the Word is going to be a comfort and joy to us, then we must read and give attention to the Word. It is not enough to read what others are saying about the Word, or to hear others preach about the Word. To receive the benefits and comfort of the Word, we must be directly involved with it.

To illustrate this point, look at Paul's famous statement to the Corinthians. "Eye hath not seen, nor ear heard, neither have entered into the heart of man, the things which God hath prepared for them that love Him" (1 Corinthians 2:9). How many times have you heard it said, based on this scripture, that heaven is so wonderful that any part of it is simply beyond the comprehension of man. Heaven is just too glorious for us to know.

Well, it is true in a sense: we can't know everything about heaven, due to our finite natures. However, when we look at the following verse of this same chapter, we readily see that much spiritual insight is available to us through the Word and the Holy Spirit. "But God hath revealed them unto us by his Spirit," Paul wrote, "for the Spirit searcheth all things, yea, the deep things of God" (1 Corinthians 2:10).

John Calvin said, "If we are to partake of the blessings of the Spirit, we must read the Word of God." There is no revelation apart from the Scriptures, for the Lord gives His people illumination *by* the Spirit *through* the Word. This means that we have no comfort of the Spirit if there is no involvement with Scripture. The Word can be very comforting and bring much joy if we will attend to it. However, if there is no Word, there will be no comfort and no joy.

The Holy Spirit works through the Word. The Word is the window and door of the Spirit, whereby He makes His entry into the heart of the believer. As the Word is in the heart of the believer, there is a source for the Holy Spirit to lay hold on and work through. The action of the Spirit, in making Christ really present to the minister, is always in connection with the Word of God. Again, if the believer is to have joy, he must attend to Scripture in a very personal way. It is very simple. To have the joy of the Lord, one must take heed to what the Word has to say.

THE RIGHT ATTITUDE

As we think about our relationship with God the Father, God the Son, and God the Holy Spirit, we will be joyful and we will keep the proper attitude.

Perhaps the book of Philippians gives the greatest insight into joy through proper attitude. In the four chapters of

Philippians, Paul mentions "joy," "rejoicing," or "gladness" at least nineteen times.

If you would look at Paul's situation, at the time of his writing this epistle, it would seem to be anything but one in which to rejoice. Paul was in a Roman prison, his case soon to come before the high court. He knew he could be acquitted or beheaded. He was chained to a Roman soldier and not permitted to preach in public. He had always wanted to visit Rome as a preacher. Now he was there as a prisoner.

In spite of all this, however, Paul overflowed with joy. The secret of his joy was attitude. Paul, in the book of Philippians, explains the mind the believer must have if he is going to experience joy: "Let this mind be in you, which was also in Christ Jesus: Who, being in the form of God, thought it not robbery to be equal with God: But made himself of no reputation, and took upon him the form of a servant, and was made in the likeness of men: And being found in fashion as a man, he humbled himself, and became obedient unto death, even the death of the cross" (Philippians 2:5-8). Paul looked at his circumstances through Christ, and not the other way around.

Paul tells us further about the mind of Christ when he tells us to think on these things: whatsoever things are *true*, whatsoever things are *honest*, whatsoever things are *just*, whatsoever things are *pure*, whatsoever things are *lovely*, and whatsoever things are *of good report* (Philippians 4:8).

Warren W. Wiersbe, in a little book, *Be Joyful*, published by Victor Books, gives four attitudes that will help maintain joy. He takes his points from the book of Philippians. First, have a single mind. Second, have a submissive mind. Third, have a spiritual mind. And fourth, have a secure mind.

These are to be ours through Christ. We can readily see Paul had joy in his ministry. So can all of us if we pursue our God-given calling with the same attitude as Paul.

KNOWING GOD PROTECTS AND DELIVERS

The joy of ministry is heightened through faith in God's providential care. "Thou art my hiding place; Thou shalt preserve me from trouble; Thou shalt compass me about with songs of deliverance. Selah" (Psalm 34:7), the psalmist wrote.

Hear Joshua say, "Have not I commanded thee? Be strong and of a good courage; be not afraid, neither be thou dismayed: for the Lord thy God is with thee whithersoever thou goest," (Joshua 1:9). Hear the psalmist again, "He that dwelleth in the secret place of the Most High shall abide under the shadow of the Almighty. I will say of the Lord, He is my refuge and my fortress: my God; in Him will I trust. Surely he shall deliver thee from the snare of the fowler, and from the noisome pestilence" (Psalm 91:1-3).

Moses told the children of Israel, "And this is the blessing of Judah: and he said, Hear, Lord, the voice of Judah, and bring him unto his people: let his hands be sufficient for him; and be Thou a help to him from his enemies" (Deuteronomy 33:7). Hear Isaiah say, "When thou passest through the waters, I will be with thee; and through the rivers, they shall not overflow thee: when thou walkest through the fire, thou shalt not be burned; neither shall the flame kindle upon thee" (Isaiah 43:2).

Jesus said, "Behold, I give unto you power to tread on serpents and scorpions, and over all the power of the enemy; and nothing shall by any means hurt you" (Luke 10:19). Paul wrote in Romans, "What shall we then say to these things? If God be for us, who can be against us?" (Romans 8:31).

This certainly does not sound like gloom and doom for the minister. It is a note of eternal joy experienced in the here and now, based on faith in God's providence. To the sincere, devoted, committed servant, there is "Joy in Ministry."

CONCLUSION

Beyond a doubt, the greatest joy for the minister comes when he helps lead someone to Christ. How exciting it is when a person repents! Seeing someone get saved brings more joy than all other events because the person who finds Christ discovers the foundation for an "abundant life."

The minister finds special joy in the salvation experience because:

1. The minister knows the new convert is now able to receive God's wonderful plan for his or her life.
2. The minister finds he is able to minister even more

effectively for the Lord because the new convert is more open to the minister's advice and counseling.

3. The minister can now see the new convert grow and become more obedient to Jesus.

4. The minister knows that as the new convert enters into a continuing life and union with God through Christ, he will open up more to God, to self, and to others.

5. The minister knows that just as he has experienced joy in ministering for Jesus, the new convert will find joy in ministry also.

The minister's joy comes from being able to participate with the new convert in all this growth and development process; thus, it is not unusual for a minister to find much joy at the conversion of others.

Our Lord tells us ". . . likewise joy shall be in heaven over one sinner that repenteth . . ." (Luke 15:7).

Yes, we can have joy in ministry. We can have it by appreciating our calling from God through Christ our Lord, as well as by recognizing God's indwelling in us through the Holy Spirit. We can have joy when everything is going smoothly or even when a crisis situation has developed. Most assuredly, we can have joy when we are leading individuals to higher ground.

"Rejoice in the Lord alway: and again I say rejoice" is not merely a statement of fact by Paul. The repetition of the word "rejoice" at the beginning and ending of this statement is what is called in the Greek "cyclus"—a circle. The repetition of what is said is a circle. This usage was often applied to a song of deliverance, of triumph after victory. What Paul is doing here is calling on others to rejoice because of the victory we have in Christ and to sing it as a continuous song.

God intended for us always to have "JOY IN MINISTRY."

7

THE ETERNAL PERSPECTIVE

James D. Jenkins

During the first six chapters our authors have portrayed the joy of ministry in excellent fashion. We have discussed the pulpit, the parsonage, the outside world, the private place, the altar, and crises counseling. Nevertheless, the joy of ministry is so prodigious that some things bear repeating, as the apostle Peter might write, in order to "stir up our pure minds by way of remembrance" (2 Peter 3:1).

Even in quiet times—at the end of day, the week, the month, or year—during times of reflection, there is more joy for the minister to discover. Just remembering we are called of God will produce gladness. Understanding that we can know His will for our life and that our ministry has eternal value brings joy unspeakable.

We ministers begin our work as a result of divine call. We continue under the guidance of the Holy Spirit. We stand fast, both on the mountaintops and in the valleys, when we realize that eternal matters rest in God's divine providence.

THE CALL

What an honor to be called, chosen, separated unto the gospel of God. Paul said it this way: "And I thank Christ Jesus, our Lord, who hath enabled me, for that he counted me faithful, putting me into the ministry" (1 Timothy 1:12).

We receive some joy from being recognized by important people, honored in various ways, but the greatest thrill that can come to any of us is to be counted worthy (or faithful) to serve Jesus Christ as our life's vocation, a vocation in which we serve both God and people with our entire being.

In terms of today's world the ministry is an honorable profession. Should one choose the ministry in this professional sense, strickly because of the "glamour" or in order to attain social status, he has decided his own calling. While one could be commended, perhaps, for having a desire to minister to people, at the same time he or she is to be pitied for being without the assurance of God's call. Every minister needs the assurance that he is chosen for this service.

Many people I know who have received the call of God have also resisted it somewhat. They knew the ministry was a worthy profession. They also knew it carried awesome responsibilities and that it meant serving—not being served. They knew that a love for mankind and a concern for the welfare of others was a prerequisite for success in the ministry and they would not even attempt to preach without first knowing they really had no choice. In other words, these men concluded without reservation that ministry was God's divine will for their lives. They knew His will is the only route to peace, contentment, joy, and fulfillment. Such men have a call and they can say with the Apostle Paul, "Woe is unto me, if I preach not the Gospel" (1 Corinthians 9:16).

Since the Lord honors and uses our individual personalities and the uniqueness of our circumstances, each call seems to be different. Isaiah was still in mourning followng the death of King Uzziah when he had an unusual encounter with God. An angel visited Isaiah, touching his lips with a live coal from the altar of God. The Lord spoke, asking, "Whom shall I send, and who will go for us?" Isaiah's first response was repentance and confession: his next response, "Here am I; send me" (Isaiah 6:1-8).

My father-in-law says that from the time he was a small boy he felt he would be a minister. He wasn't raised in church like many of us, yet this feeling was ever present, something innate. When he became an adult, though, he continually made excuses and tried to free himself of the burden. Having never shared this feeling with a certain minister friend, the minister said to my father-in-law one day, "I have two places to go for revival, scheduled for the same week. Why don't you take one of them?" My father-in-law declined but the man came to his house, got him out of bed, and asked again, "Will you go and preach the revival?" The Lord moved upon my father-in-law to go; and, as you might guess, it was a great meeting with several saved and a number baptized with the Holy Ghost. That church is still active today.

My father was actually plowing in a field when the Lord spoke and called him into the ministry. Dad told the Lord that he would not be a preacher. Instantly, something knocked him to the ground. He got up and the voice spoke to him again. Again, Dad said no and again he was knocked to the ground. This time my father submitted to the Lord's will.

I do not know what experiences or feelings my father had prior to this but, as a pioneer Church of God preacher, he had an experience that left no doubt about God's will for his life.

God's hand upon an obedient, willing individual makes a difference. When the load seems too heavy, let us remember the call and by whom we are called. The privilege of serving should always outweigh the heaviness of duty. If we make a terrible blunder, let us remember that God does not revoke the call just because we make a mistake. We should re-live our calling often and thank the Lord for it. We should also examine the way our calling is being fulfilled and treasure examples of God's call to others, as recorded in His Word.

The demands are great, the burdens are heavy, the salary is usually lower than other vocations with comparable responsibilities, but God's reward is unmeasurable. Let us therefore walk worthy of the vocation wherein we have been called (Ephesians 4:1).

Obedience to God's call brings joy!

THE ANOINTING

It has been said that preaching is the art of expressing divine truth in such terms of living beauty as shall attract and win and so save the soul. When we are called and anointed, we can say with Jeremiah, "His word was in mine heart as a burning fire shut up in my bones" (Jeremiah 20:9). The best way to have an effective pulpit manner is to have a superior soul—through praying and applying the Word—and to pour out the whole of it in our preaching.

Jeremiah said, "His word was in mine heart" (Jeremiah 20:9). I believe the Word plays a vital role in the minister's anointing and I have two excellent examples of this. My father was a real student of the word and one of the best gospel preachers I have ever heard. My father-in-law has been a reader of the word all his adult life. He is now 82 years old and, though not physically well, he still reads the Bible through seven to eight times a year. My wife says that when she thinks of her dad she usually thinks of the Word of God. If such could be said about more of us ministers, I believe we would have more anointed messages.

Many fine things have been written on anointing. Even Jesus introduced His ministry with a reference to anointing. "The Spirit of the Lord is upon me, because He hath anointed me to preach the gospel" (Luke 4:18). It is a subject which should command our attention and constant, prayerful review.

THE COMMISSIONING

Let us think back to that local church and the night we were set forth for the ministry. Those with whom we had worshiped were there. Our pastor was there. Even the Exhorter's examination which lay ahead did not diminish our enthusiasm. What a thrill! If any of that thrill has been lost, smothered by responsibilities and the routineness of life, then we need to regain that joy and find new challenge in ministry.

After all, we *were* commissioned by the Church of God and we *should* love our church. It has given us a place to exercise the call of God upon our lives. It has provided us a place of service, along with certain necessities of life but most of all the church gives us a sense of belonging.

Psychology teaches there are three significant feelings vital to self-esteem: belongingness, worthiness, and competence. The church is a place where we can experience all three. At considerable sacrifice, the church provides educational opportunities, seminars, and state and national meetings where we can belong, become more worthy, and achieve competence. Those who value their call from God and their commissioning by the church return loyalty in the name of the Master.

THE EQUIPMENT

Each of us has been given talents from the Lord. The fact that we accepted the call proves that we did not simply hide our talent as the man of whom Jesus spoke (Matthew 25:24). As we continue to multiply our talents, putting them to Kingdom use, we will discover added joy.

One of the minister's *most* vital assets is a good name. The wise man wrote, "A good name is rather to be chosen than great riches" (Proverbs 22:1a). We all begin life with a good name. We have no reputation when we are born and it is up to us to keep our name unmarred. People in the congregation and in the community are always watching us. They will not justify our actions so readily as we ourselves, so we must be careful.

Learning to live within our income is also a great asset. We are stewards of what God has entrusted to our care and we will be more highly respected as we exhibit caution and responsibility in the area of personal and church finances. Not only do we and our family members benefit from a good name in the church and in the community, but our congregation will also gain much satisfaction from hearing others express confidence in us and knowing they can speak with pride about their pastor.

Something else which every preacher desperately needs is a finely tuned sense of humor.

It has been said, "Life is only worth living if you have a sense of humor." Who can define humor? It is a mood, an inclination, an atmosphere. Try to mold humor into a definition, and it escapes you. Try to force it into a contrast, and it disappears. Try to analyze it, and it ceases to be humor. We should remember, though, that humor is not buffoonery. Good humor is full of emotion, sympathy, optimism. Humor takes the pain from blame and adapts itself to every climate of life. So, the preacher must see to it that his life is sprinkled with humor.

Humor and humanity go together, and the preacher who lacks one generally lacks the other! "Nature and humor cannot be far apart." The source and spring of humor is human life itself. Let humor touch the style, the face, the manner of the preacher, and men at once recognize a power that attracts them. Humor is infectious. Never has there been a popular minister in day-to-day affairs and a popular preacher in the pulpit, in the best sense of the word, who did not possess humor.

Some men are cursed with gloom and despair because they cannot laugh at life or at themselves. It is a drudgery to be around ministers who are obsessed with their own distorted sense of importance. They are unable to relax, or to laugh, or to find pleasure in the ordinary events of life. Some preachers really have qualities of greatness yet never fulfill their potential or do their best work because they lack humor and warmth.

We can clothe ourselves in all manner of vestments and positions, but men simply will not recognize apostolic succession. We should not take ourselves too seriously and we should remember that being human can go a long way toward making others comfortable in our presence. Humor has been defined as a mixture of love and wit. American humor, like our national character, is of no distinct type. We make fun of everything. Perhaps this, then, is the first service of humor, to bring the preacher into touch with his family, his congregation, and his fellow ministers. Humor is humanity. No task on earth requires us to be more human than that of ministry.

THE PLACE OF SERVICE

". . .I have learned, in whatsoever state I am, therewith to be content" (Philippians 4:11). Paul learned this because he kept his eyes on Christ. "For me to live is Christ," Paul wrote (Philippians 1:21). Jesus Christ was everything to Paul, the joy of his life. We cannot be filled with the pursuit of worldly things and filled with Jesus Christ at the same time. Being content is completely opposite to striving. Contentment can be found only in seeking first the kingdom of God (Matthew 6:33).

Wherever we are serving—whether it be as an evangelist, as an associate pastor, pastor, missionary, or administrator—we are each part of the body of Christ. We each have a unique role and function in His kingdom and love for the Master makes us willing to sacrifice in His name.

When the Apostle Paul gave himself to Jesus Christ, he

turned his back on position and income. It was a step of faith and commitment. He earned at least part of his livelihood as a tentmaker, but he certainly did not enjoy the luxury which had been afforded him from birth. Nevertheless, Paul knew the meaning of contentment.

For every minister there will be sacrifices. We will occasionally experience loneliness and we may feel we would like to be closer to family members. In my own early years of pastoring, my wife, daughter, and I could generally be rather content for we realized living away from family was just part of the ministry. However, on the eve of one of those early Christmases my wife felt unusually lonesome. All the church members were with their families. We felt isolated, cut off, and we talked about it. Shortly, there was a knock on the door. Some of our church members had stopped by for a visit. Those wonderful people will never know what they meant to us that Christmas Eve.

When we trust God, He supplies our needs. He even provides those who become as close as family members. In all our years of pastoring, that one occasion was about the extent of our feeling such a loss. It isn't always possible for us to live near parents, brothers, sisters, children, and grandchildren—and this is truly a sacrifice—but we can still have joy in the Lord. God has given us "family" everywhere we have lived. We can learn to be peaceful and content, thoroughly involved in loving relationships, even when blood relatives live miles away.

While this may not always be so—the story of Abraham and Isaac is a beautiful example of how God sometimes requires only a willingness to sacrifice—God will teach us that true happiness and joy comes only with being in His will.

In all places of service, let us offer sacrifices of praise, thanksgiving, and love:

> "Rejoice in the Lord alway: and again I say rejoice. Let your moderation be known unto all men. The Lord is at hand. Be careful for nothing; but in every thing by prayer and supplication with thanksgiving let your requests be made known unto God. And the peace of God, which passeth all understanding, shall keep your hearts and minds through Christ Jesus. Finally, brethren, whatsoever things are true, whatsoever things are honest, whatsoever things are just, whatsoever things are pure,

whatsoever things are lovely, whatsoever things are of good report; if there be any virtue, and if there be any praise, think on these things" (Philippians 4:4-8).

An unwavering determination to do our very best for God, wherever we are placed, will create satisfaction, inspire contentment, and bring joy. Our true place of service is always God's place of choice.

THE PROVIDENCE OF GOD

God is not only a God of redemption, but He is also a God of providence. In the providence of God, He called us. What joy this realization brings. In His providence He anointed us to preach the Gospel. He did not redeem us and then leave us. He did not forsake us after He called us. He is ever with us, present through all experiences.

What is divine providence? It is that care whereby the Creator preserves all His creatures. Everything is in God's control: all power is His. He makes all things—physical, mental, and moral—to conform to His purpose. Not only does He "uphold all things by the word of His power" (Hebrews 1:3) but He makes us "more than conquerors" (Romans 8:37) through Jesus Christ our Lord. God is not merely a silent spectator of human affairs. He is involved. If He suspended His influence and withdrew His hand, the system of nature would dissolve into nothingness.

"God is the judge, He putteth down one and setteth up another" (Psalm 75:7). He governs the successes and failures of men. We are not lost in the crowd. Our work is not in vain: therein is joy! When we know God so well that nothing can make us doubt Him or His promises, when we continue to develop complete trust in Him, as Judge and as the impartial "promoter" of man, then our energies will be spent walking worthy of His divine call.

The story of Jacob and Joseph is well known. Jacob showed partiality and that partiality produced jealousy which caused Joseph's brothers to want to kill him. However, God directed and a lesser evil was committed. God slowly unveiled His plan for Joseph's life.

"And Jacob rent his clothes and put sackcloth upon his loins, and mourned for his son many days" (Genesis 37:34). ". . .but he refused to be comforted" (Genesis 37:35). ". . . Jacob said to his sons, why do ye look one upon another?" (Genesis 42:1b).

Through those very things against which Jacob cried in his despair, God in His infinite wisdom brought about His wonderful plan with far-reaching purposes and eternal benefits. Joseph's brothers sold him into slavery. Jealousy was their motive. Joseph came to understand the providence of God. Later, he told his brothers, ". . . for God did send me before you."

Such examples of how God turns things around and uses evil plans to accomplish His eternal purposes should encourage us daily. God's blessings are often camouflaged. We know not what is of man and what is of God. God's blessings are often veiled, with only time unfolding them to those of us who look for His blessings. We have not had, nor will we ever have, a trial or difficulty which surprises God. He sees the sparrow's flight and fall. He calls the stars by name. He clothes the lily of the field. Of how much more value is each of us. "He will perfect that which concerneth me," the psalmist wrote (Psalm 138:8).

Some difficulties arise from our failing to seek His will. Some men live as if they are in charge of their own fate, master of their own souls. They act as if they control and are in charge of what is happening in their lives. No one in the ministry thinks that, but let us beware that our actions do not hint at such. Our daily plans should be laid with His will in mind. James reminds us: "For that ye ought to say, If the Lord will, we shall live, and do this, or that" (James 4:15).

James further reminds us we "know not what shall be on the morrow. For what is your life? It is even a vapour, that appeareth for a little time, and then vanisheth away" (James 4:14). However, life is a vapour in the hands of God. We must realize the brevity of life. We certainly must not procrastinate. Our work is important. It has eternal value. One life can accomplish much when yielded to His control.

The very thing which seems so crushing, disappointing, difficult, and mountainous—God makes to work for us. Can you not recall incidents which momentarily crushed you? Yet later proved beneficial? Some of my biggest disappointments have turned out to be spiritual stepping stones. In order to see the way clearly we must keep our eyes on Him. Paul wrote, "For our light affliction worketh for us a far more exceeding and eternal weight of glory" (2 Corinthians 4:17). He went on to say, "While we look not at the things which are seen, but at the things which are not seen: for the things which are seen are temporal; but the things which are not seen are eternal" (2 Corinthians 4:18).

I love to mediate on the words of a song written over two hundred years ago;

> God moves in a mysterious way
>   His wonders to perform;
> He plants His footsteps in the sea,
>   And rides upon the storm.
>
> Deep in unfathomable mines,
>   With never-failing skill,
> He treasures up His bright designs,
>   And works His sovereign will.
>
> Ye fearful saints, fresh courage take;
>   The clouds ye so much dread
> Are big with mercy, and shall break
>   In blessings on your head.

THE WILL OF GOD

The most valuable life is one seeking to live in harmony with the will of God. We must remain ever conscious of the need to be in God's will. Right where we are, where providence has placed us—this may be where we will do the best for God. In the will of God we can live a life of obedience and victory no matter the conditions or circumstances. God would have us be faithful. One of the highest compliments we pay a man is to say, "You can depend on him."

The most important guide for knowing God's will is the Bible. Although God uses the indwelling Holy Spirit to lead us, and although He uses circumstances to reveal His will, it is the Bible which remains the foundation for all spiritual guidance. The Holy Spirit never prompts us to do something which disagrees with the Word. He will not tell us to do bizarre things. To search elsewhere before we look to God's Word for His will is wasted effort. Let us also remember that the Word should always be studied in context.

You, no doubt have heard the story of the man who decided to open the Bible at random. First he read, "Judas went and hanged himself." Thinking he could get more specific direction, he randomly opened the Bible again and read, "Go thou and do likewise." A third time he opened the Bible and was dismayed when his eyes fell upon the words: "What thou doest, do quickly."

Although a humorous story, it certainly makes a point. In spite of all the times when a single Bible passage has proven an inspiration we must study God's Word seriously and in context. A contractor could never build a house by reading only isolated sections of the blueprint. Nor could a mechanic work on our automobiles nor a doctor care for our bodies if either used their instructional guides in this fashion.

We can evaluate life from the human perspective and feel doomed, or we can meet it with faith and soar like the eagle. Our relationship with God is the key. If we believe He is guiding our footsteps, we will not complain and afflict others with our troubles.

The story is told of a man who fell from a wagon he was driving. The horses went wild but he managed to hold on to the reigns. Neighbors yelled for him to turn loose. The man held on and was dragged along the road until almost dead. He finally got the horses stopped. People gathered around, still wondering why he hadn't turned loose. Just before he died, the man gasped, "Look inside the wagon." Inside the wagon was his little baby girl.

As parents, most of us feel certain we would have done the same thing; but that brings us to another question. If we aren't required to die for our children, are we willing to really LIVE for them? They know if we face life with a defeated attitude or if we soar in faith like the eagle. Do our lives reflect the importance of His will?

Holy Scripture indicates that God leads men to know His will through a variety of ways. The following list of methods is exemplary, not exhaustive. God leads us:

1. *Through the Word* (Joshua 1:7, 8; Colossians 3:16; Isaiah 8:20). Men have always referred to the Scriptures for guidance and direction for their lives.

2. *Through reason* (Isaiah 1:18; Acts 6:2). God's ways are not always known to man, but they are not generally contrary to sound reason.

3. *Through persuasion* (Jeremiah 44:4; Zechariah 7:7). God uses persuasion to bring men to Him in reconciliation, but He also leads us in terms of earthly decisions as well.

4. *Through inner checks and restraints* (Acts 16:6-8). Paul was sensitive to this inner spiritual indication of God's will.

5. *Through open and/or closed doors* (1 Corinthians 16:9; Galatians 4:20). Not every open door or perceived opportunity is God's will for our life but He does move in this way.

6. *Through inclination of heart and mind* in one direction rather than another (1 Kings 8:58; Psalm 119:36; Proverbs 21:1; 2 Corinthians 8:16). God also will see that evil men submit to do His will (2 Kings 19:28; Isaiah 45:1-6; Revelation 17:1).

Through dreams and visions (Matthew 2:13, 19, 10; Acts 16:9, 10; 22:17, 18).

Remember, God's timetable is not as ours. Being the sovereign God He may choose to frustrate our best laid plans. The Bible clearly indicates that some things come only by prayer. If we neglect prayer, we will miss these things. Therefore, let us submit everything to Him in prayer that He might direct our lives for our good and His glory. Prayer and the Word are primary keys for knowing the will of God.

Let us keep in mind that our disappointments may be His appointments. What joy to sing with all sincerity, "Where He Leads Me I Will Follow."

THE CHRISTIAN FELLOWSHIP

Not only does the minister have a blessed fellowship with his family, as discussed in chapter two, but there is joy of companionship—a manly fellowship—among colleagues who follow the Master. Petty jealousy may sometimes intrude but, on the whole, the fellowship and camaradery of ministers is more frank, genial, rich in substance, happy in expression, and practical in mutual service than in any other profession. Herein is a constant and noble joy for all of us.

We tend to use the word "friendship" quite loosely. Much that is termed friendship really has not earned the label. Generally there are three things which generate friendship: good times, money, and integrity. The first two of these do not usually produce genuine friendship. When money and pleasures fade, so does the friendship. As small children we learned that in the story of the prodigal son.

Jonathan and David exemplify real friendship. They had harmony in the love of virtue and the fear of God. Real friendship is more loving rather than being loved. It is doing what is best for the other, with sincerity as its foundation. We need the ability to see things from another's point of view, to get "in his shoes," to "look out the windows of his heart." An old proverb says, "Shared sorrow is half sorrow but shared joy is double joy." Stable friendships come out of common tasks and common goals.

Jonathan and David had an ultimate friendship: "And it came to pass, when he had made an end of speaking unto Saul, that the soul of Jonathan was KNIT with the soul of David, and Jonathan loved him as his own soul" (1 Samuel 18:1). If there was a man in all Israel who had reason to be jealous of David, it was Prince Jonathan. He was heir to the throne and he would be "supplanted" by David. In David, Jonathan could see and admire what a leader in Israel should be. Let us strive to be as worthy of a good man's friendship as was David of Jonathan's.

Paul said that his friend Onesiphorus refreshed him. His friend was like a breath of fresh air. Have we become too sophisticated to show our friends how much they mean to us? Have we let evils of this world restrain us from showing affection, for fear of being "labeled?" Friends are among our most valuable possessions and we ought to cultivate and value them at all times.

The best example on how to make and keep friends is surely found in Paul's letter to the Corinthians. He tells us love is longsuffering, it does not envy, does not seek her own, is not easily provoked, thinketh no evil, rejoiceth in the truth. Love never fails. Without love, we are nothing (1 Corinthians 13).

Friendships are important enough to cultivate and not abandon quickly. My wife and I have had some friends for several years. At one point a slight difference of opinion arose, threatening to develop into a wider breach. Rebecca and I discussed the situation, confirming with each other that too much effort had gone into the friendship, and that it was far too valuable, to forsake. If more friends would determine that friendships should last just as marriages should last, our joy would be even greater.

Jesus is a friend who sticketh closer than a brother. His love is without beginning, without intermission, and without end, from everlasting to everlasting. What joy!

Here are some further examples of what the Bible says of friendship: (Proverbs 18:24; 27:6a; 27:10).

THE EXAMPLE OF OTHERS

We owe a debt to those who have labored before us in ministry and we have the privilege of receiving wisdom which is the result of their successes and disappointments. Many of these men and women have set before us outstanding examples. In addition to this knowledge handed down to us, we have the joy and privilege of passing along what we have gained from our own experiences.

As with Elijah and Elisha, the young are to take up the work which the older are laying down. One workman passes from the scene of action but the work goes on. Somehow it gives us a sense of marching with the dead who cannot really die, making us strive for a faith that others would desire as a double portion (2 Kings 2:9).

Clergymen aren't the only ones with strong faith, of course. What a privilege to work with men and women in our local churches. When my wife, daughter, and I got to our first church, after leaving Lee College, the first individuals we met were three young couples who had a dedication and a faith that equalled that of many ministers. Regardless of the sacrifice, they had a determination to work for the Lord and His church. At that first church I also quickly became appreciative of the advice and counsel of an older brother who had been there for a number of years. When he died, I felt lost and found myself wishing the Lord had left him longer because I had depended upon his wisdom.

Thank God for the way He uses men and women to help in our work for Him. John Wesley said, "I will not only defend the faith myself, but I will organize so that uncounted thousands, and millions even, may take care of the faith when I am gone and forgotten." What John Wesley didn't know was that he will never be forgotten. What a wise man to organize in this fashion for the Gospel's sake!

Though we often grieve at the thought of our "Elijahs" leaving us, it is well also that we not delay expressing our appreciation and gratitude. We should remember such men on birthdays and other special occasions. The debt we owe to these men is too large to repay, but we can at least make an effort to show appreciation for where they have brought this church.

CONCLUSION

Change is such a part of our world and our work. People move away. Others move in. The one thing of which we can be certain is change. Our children grow up and leave home. We see those children to whom we have ministered grow to adulthood. We see lives change for the better or for the worse. In light of all this constant change, it is comforting to know that the results of our kingdom work are eternal. What is done for Christ will last.

Some members and friends of the church seem to think that a minister never has difficulties, that he somehow lives in a flower garden, but we must ever be on guard, keeping in mind that no matter what good has been accomplished through all our ministerial activities, and no matter how much joy we have created for others and experienced ourselves, we are in warfare with the enemy. The Apostle Paul said, "Lest I myself be a castaway" (1 Corinthians 9:28). Paul understood the possible danger of his becoming a worthless guide to the unsearchable riches of Christ. He knew that it is possible for a man to lead others into the heavenly way and yet lose the way himself. What a tragedy. We must determine to remain victorious, to trust our Christ, never wavering.

"Whether therefore you eat, or drink, or whatsoever ye do, do all to the glory of God" (1 Corinthians 10:31). We are sometimes tempted to measure faithfulness by the amount of ground we cover, the number of things we get done: however, faithfulness also requires making time for prayer, study of the Word, devotional reading, and self-examination. Otherwise, the minister runs the risk of being overtaken with activity while losing sight of true values. Not the one who runs the fastest but the one who endures until the end will be saved.

In the midst of all these activities—the pulpit, the parsonage, the altar—grace abounds! The joy of the Lord is our strength. The realization that we are helping people as we pass this way, that our living is not in vain—this is worth everything.

We determine to see Jesus, to hear Him say, "Well done thy good and faithful servant." And this is joy indeed!

Samuel Shoemaker was a pastor who died in 1963. Near the end of his life he wrote, "An Apologia for My Life," words with which I wish to close this book. Here is how Sam described the work of a minister. His words seem applicable especially in terms of the "Joy of Ministry."

I Stay Near the Door

I stay near the door.
I neither go too far in, nor stay too far out,
The door is the most important door in the world—
It is the door through which men walk when they find God.
There's no use my going way inside, and staying there,
When so many are still outside and they, as much as I,
Crave to know where the door is.
And all that so many ever find
Is only the wall where a door ought to be.
They creep along the wall like blind men,
With outstretched, groping hands,
Feeling for a door, knowing there must be a door,
Yet they never find it . . .
So I stay near the door.

The most tremendous thing in the world
Is for men to find that door—the door to God.
The most important thing any man can do
Is to take hold of one of those blind, groping hands,
And put it on the latch—the latch that only clicks
And opens to the man's own touch.
Men die outside that door, as starving beggars die
On cold nights in cruel cities in the dead of winter—

Die for want of what is within their grasp.
They live, on the other side of it—live because they have
    found it.
Nothing else matters compared to helping them find it,
And open it, and walk in, and find Him . . .
So I stay near the door.

Go in, great saints, go all the way in—
Go way down into the cavernous cellars,
And way up into the spacious attics—
It is a vast, roomy house, this house where God is.
Go into the deepest of hidden casements,
Of withdrawal, of silence, of sainthood.
Some must inhabit those inner rooms,
And know the depths and heights of God,
And call outside to the rest of us how wonderful it is.
Sometimes I take a deeper look in,
Sometimes venture in a little farther;
But my place seems closer to the opening . . .
So I stay near the door.

There is another reason why I stay there.
Some people get part way in and become afraid
Lest God and the zeal of His house devour them,
For God is so very great, and asks all of us.
And these people feel a cosmic claustrophobia,
And want to get out. "Let me out!" they cry.
And the people way inside only terrify them more.
Somebody must be by the door to tell them that they are
    spoiled
For the old life, they have seen too much:
Once taste God, and nothing but God will do any more.
Somebody must be watching for the frightened
Who seek to sneak out just where they came in,
To tell them how much better it is inside.

The people too far in do not see how near these are
To leaving—preoccupied with the wonder of it all.
Somebody must watch for those who have entered the door
But would like to run away. So for them, too,
I stay near the door.
I admire the people who go way in.
But I wish they would not forget how it was
Before they got in. Then they would be able to help
The people who have not yet even found the door,
Or the people who want to run away again from God.

You can go in too deeply, and stay in too long,
And forget the people outside the door.
As for me, I shall take my old accustomed place.
Near enough to God to hear Him, and know He is there,
But not so far from men as not to hear them,
And remember they are there, too.

Where? Outside the door—
Thousands of them, millions of them.
But—more important for me—
One of them, two of them, ten of them,
Whose hands I am intended to put on the latch.
So I shall stay by the door and wait
For those who seek it.
"I had rather be a door-keeper . . ."
So I stay near the door.